Date Due

MR 12 '96			

Twayne's United States Authors Series

Sylvia E. Bowman, *Editor*

INDIANA UNIVERSITY

Eugene V. Debs

TUSAS 267

Eugene V. Debs

EUGENE V. DEBS

By HAROLD W. CURRIE

Michigan State University

TWAYNE PUBLISHERS
A DIVISION OF G. K. HALL & CO., BOSTON

Library of Congress Cataloging in Publication Data

Currie, Harold W.
   Eugene V. Debs.

   (Twayne's United States authors series; TUAS 267)
   Bibliography: p. 151–54.
   Includes index.
   1. Debs, Eugene Victor, 1855–1926.
HX84.D3C87   335′.3′0924 [B]   76-3780
   ISBN 0-8057-7167-0

Contents

About the Author

Harold W. Currie was educated at Tufts University, Boston University, and the University of Michigan where he received a doctor of philosophy degree in 1960. He has been a member of the staff of the William L. Clements Library at the University of Michigan and the Connecticut Historical Society. He has taught American History at the University of Connecticut and Muskingum College, and he is presently professor of American Thought and Language at Michigan State University. Professor Currie's articles and reviews have appeared in a number of scholarly journals including *The American Historical Review, Labor History, The Historian, Mid-America* and *Michigan History.*

Preface

Eugene V. Debs is easily the most famous Socialist that this country, not noted for enshrining Socialists among its heroes, has produced. Norman Thomas's name is perhaps more familiar to readers of this volume, but Thomas had the bad fortune to lead the Socialist party during its decline, while Debs was prominent during the first two decades of this century when the Socialist movement reached its peak in the United States. As an orator of considerable ability, he possessed a magnetism that attracted great crowds wherever he spoke during his five presidential campaigns between 1900 and 1920. Socialists loved him, but one did not need to agree with his radical ideas to appreciate him for the great orator and friend of the suffering masses that he was.

Debs is not as well known for his writing as he is for his speaking, but he wrote voluminously. In addition to his speeches, he turned out hundreds of articles in which he set forth the ideas to which he was devoted. Some of the articles were published separately as pamphlets; and the only book to come from his pen was *Walls and Bars,* a collection of articles on prison reform originally written as single pieces. Unfortunately, his oratorical power was not matched by his ability with a pen; his written material is frequently repetitious, and he often employed sentimentalism and flowery language to present ideas lacking in profundity. There is, however, another way of looking at his literary productions: they were colorful, direct, uncomplicated, aimed at the common man rather than at the scholar. In short, Debs was a propagandist, not a great thinker; and he never pretended to be anything else. His main objective was to spread Socialist ideas to the people during what he perceived to be a massive educational campaign. And, inasmuch as millions of Americans were exposed to these ideas in oratory and in print over three decades, they assume an importance that cannot be ignored by any student of the American experience.

Debs's career can be divided into two major phases: pre-Socialist and Socialist. Developing in a manner that is the reverse of the experience of most people, he expressed ideas prior to his conversion to Socialism that tend to be relatively conservative—and some rather surprisingly so to those who are familiar with his later views. Although I concentrate in this volume on the ideas of his more important Socialist phase, I do not neglect the earlier ideas, not only because the book would be incomplete without them, but because seeds of his later thought are present in the more conservative period.

No reader of Debs can fail to be impressed by certain ideas and attitudes that come through powerfully in his works. Above all is his deep and sincere concern for his fellow man, especially the victims of poverty and discrimination. No quality is more prominent in his writings than this intense humanism which was easily the primary motivating factor in his life. He devoted the last three decades of his career to spreading the gospel of Socialism only because he was convinced that it was the system that would most benefit mankind.

Closely associated with this compassion for his fellow man is a second quality that pervades his writing: an irrepressible optimism. This attitude is all the more remarkable in view of the many defeats which he had to face. Twice imprisoned, five times defeated for the presidency of the United States, frequently ill, and the champion of a cause that repelled the great majority of Americans, Debs seemed possessed of a superhuman spirit that would not allow defeat to stop him.

Debs's optimistic faith in his fellow man and in the efficacy of Socialism was a source of weakness as well as strength. He simply had too much confidence in the Socialist system. The economic solution—public ownership of the means of production and distribution—would by itself, he seemed to feel, create the necessary moral change in man to bring about the virtual elimination of social and economic problems. The experience of Socialist governments since Debs's time would seem to refute his claims. Although it should be pointed out in Debs's defense that his particular brand of Socialism has never really been tried, it seems obvious that whatever merit Debsian Socialism might have, it would never effect the miraculous cure of society's ills that Debs claimed for it. Debs's too simplistic solution has left him open to the charge of naïveté. And naïveté is perhaps most apparent in his failure to understand fully the racial problem, and in his belief that Socialism would so transform mankind that prisons would no longer be necessary.

While Debs unquestionably claimed too much for Socialism, he should not be dismissed as an eccentric crank—a visionary who turned away from reality. Not all of his ideas can be so easily cast aside. Although the United States still is a long way from Socialism, it has moved leftward in the years since Debs's death, and many planks of the early Socialist platforms have been enacted into law. In the field of organized labor, the industrial unionism, which he pioneered in the 1890's with his American Railway Union and which he championed so ardently throughout his life, is now very much a reality. While such influence is difficult to prove, the ideas that Debs hammered home for thirty years must have had a considerable impact.

My study of Debs's writings has led me to the conclusion that he stood for fundamental ideas that were very definitely in the American tradition. This view is no doubt contrary to the belief of most Americans who tend to regard all forms of Socialism as "un-American." A thorough consideration of all the reasons for this hostility cannot be attempted here, but one very powerful factor in such an attitude is undoubtedly the perversion of Socialism that has been perpetrated in the Soviet Union since 1917. Although Debs welcomed the Russian Revolution, he deplored the developments that followed it; and he undoubtedly would have condemned the crimes of Stalin had he been living during the 1930's. Certainly the differences between Communism as it has developed in the Soviet Union and Debsian Socialism overshadow the similarities. On the other hand, the fundamental principles behind Debsian Socialism and Americanism are the same, for both profess a belief in equality, individual freedom, and democracy. The gap between them arises from the fact that Americans have not always adhered to these fundamental beliefs. To cite only one obvious example, the attitude of white Americans toward Blacks makes a mockery of all of these principles. The fact that most Americans did not practice what they preached made Debsian Socialism necessary. Debs's call for public ownership of the means of production and distribution was an extension of the principle of democracy into the economic realm. The elimination of the wealthy capitalist would narrow the gap between rich and poor and promote economic and social equality. With the elimination of poverty would come a greater freedom for the individual. Thus, if one goes to the roots, one discovers that the fundamental ideas behind Americanism and Debsian Socialism are identical; the difference in the two systems results from the fact that Debs continued to be governed by these principles while Americans generally have been content to pay lip service to them.

It is not the intent of the publishers of this series to produce full-scale biographies, and I make no pretense of having done so. Debs has been honored by a biography commensurate with his stature. *The Bending Cross* by Ray Ginger is one of the finest biographies that has ever been written about an American, and it has been invaluable to me in the preparation of this book. I have relied heavily on it for the facts of Debs's life, but my treatment of his ideas rests on an examination of Debs's writings themselves rather than on secondary sources. My approach to Debs's writing differs somewhat from that of most of the authors in this series; for, since Debs wrote no major works, I have not analyzed single works at length but have organized my book around ideas. Neither have I attempted to assess the sources of Debs's ideas, for to do so would necessitate another book-length study. My intent is to provide for the reader a brief but comprehensive discussion of Debs's ideas, both major and minor, with emphasis on those ideas and attitudes that are most significant in understanding the man and his thought.

I would like to express my appreciation to all who assisted me in the preparation of this book. The staffs of the following libraries were especially helpful: State Historical Society of Wisconsin; Milwaukee County Historical Society; Indiana State Library; Debs House, Terre Haute; Lilly Library, Indiana University; University of Michigan Library; Michigan State University Library. I am also indebted to Sylvia Bowman, editor of this series, who suggested that I write the book. All-University Research Grants from Michigan State University furnished essential financial assistance. *Mid-America*, where part of Chapter 8 originally appeared in slightly different form, has graciously allowed me to reprint it here. Finally, my deepest gratitude goes to the three women in my life: my mother, Jennie Winslow Currie, who provided encouragement throughout and meticulously proofread all of my copy; my mother-in-law, Mary Benson Jackson, whose reminiscences about life as a prominent Socialist's daughter were the original stimulus for my study of American Socialism; my wife, Mary Jackson Currie, who prepared the index and whose shining optimism and cheerful acceptance of the strange moods and frequent absences that surround the writing of a book helped me through the most difficult times.

HAROLD W. CURRIE

Michigan State University

Chronology

1855 Eugene Victor Debs born November 5, in Terre Haute, Indiana; the first son of Jean Daniel and Marguerite Marie Bettrich Debs.

1870 May 23, went to work for the Terre Haute and Indianapolis Railway Company; first, as a laborer; later, as a locomotive fireman.

1874 Left railroad and became a billing clerk.

1875 Joined and became secretary of the newly organized local of the Brotherhood of Locomotive Firemen.

1878 Became associate editor of the *Locomotive Firemen's Magazine.*

1879 Elected to a two-year term as city clerk of Terre Haute.

1880 July 18, became grand secretary and treasurer of the Brotherhood of Locomotive Firemen and editor of the *Locomotive Firemen's Magazine.*

1881 Reelected to another two-year term as city clerk of Terre Haute.

1884 Elected to the Indiana House of Representatives as a Democrat.

1885 June 9, married to Katherine Metzel.

1892 September, resigned as secretary-treasurer of the Brotherhood of Locomotive Firemen; remained as editor.

1893 June 20, American Railway Union formed with Debs as president.

1894 April, American Railway Union victorious in strike against the Great Northern Railroad. May–July, Pullman Strike; Debs arrested for his part in the strike and sentenced to six months in jail. September, resigned as editor of the *Locomotive Firemen's Magazine.*

1895	November 22, released after serving his term in the McHenry County Jail, Woodstock, Illinois.
1896	Supported William Jennings Bryan and the Populists in the presidential campaign.
1897	January 1, announced his conversion to Socialism. June, American Railway Union dissolved, and members founded the Social Democracy of America with Debs as chairman.
1898	Split in the Social Democracy of America resulted in the founding of the Social Democratic party which Debs supported.
1900	Received 96,978 votes as presidential nominee of the Social Democratic party.
1901	The Socialist Party of America founded.
1904	Received 402,460 votes as presidential nominee of the Socialist Party of America.
1905	June, participated in the founding of the Industrial Workers of the World.
1907	Joined the staff of the *Appeal to Reason.*
1908	Received 420,793 votes as presidential nominee of the Socialist Party of America.
1912	Received 897,011 votes, six percent of the total, in the most successful Socialist presidential campaign in American history.
1913	Resigned from the *Appeal to Reason.*
1914	Became editorial writer and lecturer for the *National Rip-Saw.*
1916	Declined to run for President. Defeated in attempt to secure election to Congress from his home district in Indiana.
1918	June 16, delivered anti-war speech in Canton, Ohio. June 30, arrested for violation of the Espionage Act. September 14, sentenced to ten years in prison.
1919	April, began serving sentence at West Virginia State Penitentiary at Moundsville. June, transferred to federal prison, Atlanta, Georgia.
1920	While still in prison, nominated by Socialists to be their presidential candidate for fifth time; received 919,000 votes, his highest total, although a smaller percentage of the vote than in 1912.
1921	December 25, released from prison by President Warren G. Harding.

1922 Prepared a series of articles about his prison experiences; later published them as *Walls and Bars*. October 8, announced that he would reject the entreaties of the Communists to join them and would remain with the Socialist party.

1926 October 20, passed away at Lindlahr Sanitarium, Elmhurst, Illinois.

1927 *Walls and Bars* published.

CHAPTER 1

Before the Conversion

ONE of the outstanding facts of Eugene Debs's life is the love and admiration that he received even from those who deplored his ideas. "There was more of goodness in him than bubbled up in any other American of his day," wrote journalist Heywood Broun after Debs's death.[1] And Robert Hunter, a writer who belonged to the Socialist party, once had this to say about the Socialist leader:

Ask anyone. Go to the poor, the vagrant, the hobo. Go to the churches, to the rich, to the banker, to the traction magnate. You will find that every single one will say that 'Gene has something which other men do not possess. Some will say he is rash, unwise, and too radical. Others will say that he is too good for this world, and that his visions and dreams are the fanciful outpourings of a generous but impractical soul. But ask them about his character, his honesty, his sincerity, and unconsciously many of them will remove their hats.[2]

No other facets of Debs are more significant or do more to explain his success and the success of the American Socialist movement in the early twentieth century.

I *The Early Years*

The high esteem in which Debs was held by many throughout his life began at an early age. In Terre Haute, Indiana, where he was born on November 5, 1855, his generosity, kindliness, and willingness to be helpful made him one of the best-liked boys in town.[3] His parents, Jean Daniel and Marguerite Marie Bettrich Debs, had come to America from Alsace only six years before his birth and had settled into the grocery business in Terre Haute. Imbued with a love of the French and German Romantic writers, the father named his first son after two of them, Eugène Sue and Victor Hugo.

17

Debs inherited his father's love of learning; but, like so many schoolchildren, he found it difficult to sustain interest in the "three R's" which were the mainstay of formal education in mid-nineteenth century America. He much preferred to listen to his father read from the works of Hugo, Jean Baptiste Racine, Pierre Corneille, and Johann Wolfgang von Goethe—writers who had an important influence on his life and thought. He was especially impressed by Hugo, and Debs's subsequent writings and speeches are replete with references to the French Romantic. "Victor Hugo prophesied that the present century would abolish poverty," Debs wrote in 1903. "He was gifted with prescient vision. He foresaw the day when all the earth would be fair and beautiful and all mortals brethren, and the dawn gilded his noble brow, fired his soul with passion and inspired his pen with immortality."[4]

During Debs's school years, he worked as a clerk in his father's store during his free time, but he found the work boring. Much more attractive was the railroad; and in 1870, at the age of fourteen, he left high school, to the chagrin of his parents, and went to work for the Vandalia Railroad. Cleaning grease from the trucks of passenger coaches for fifty cents a day was something less than the glamorous job about which the youthful Debs had dreamed; but, within a short time, he graduated to painter and, ultimately, in 1871, became a fireman. Layoffs resulting from the panic of 1873 shortened his association with the Vandalia; but, determined to remain a railroader, he journeyed to St. Louis where he secured another job as a fireman. This one was also to be short-lived, however. His mother had always worried about him in what was then an extremely hazardous occupation; and in 1874, after the death of a friend beneath the wheels of a locomotive, Debs gave up the job and returned to Terre Haute.[5]

His career as a railroader, although brief, was important to his life, for it gave him a taste of the life of a workingman which he would never forget. And it had taken him to St. Louis during a depression where he had seen firsthand the misery and squalor under which too many people lived. Coupled with a fundamental concern for humanity—a respect for the freedom and dignity of man inherited from his father—these experiences were powerful influences that governed his life for years to come.

For a time Debs must have felt that his destiny was fixed unalterably to the grocery business. His next job after leaving the railroad was as a billing clerk at Hulman and Cox in Terre Haute. The fact that this was the largest wholesale grocery house in the Midwest did not ease the pain of clerking for Debs. It was no better than it had been in his father's store. And the railroad still beckoned. He continued to associate with railroad men; and, when the Grand Master of the two-year-old Brotherhood of Locomotive Firemen came to Terre Haute on an organizing trip, Debs not only joined the Brotherhood but was elected secretary of the newly founded local lodge. At the age of twenty, his long association with the cause of labor had begun.

In spite of Debs's early departure from formal schooling, he never relinquished the love of learning that his father had stimulated in him. Even while working as a fireman, he managed to attend business college for a while and never ceased reading. His engineer, with whom he roomed, tells of Debs reading far into the night. At the time, the engineer considered Debs to be "a damn fool" but changed his mind many years later: "I still believe there was a damned fool in that room, but I know now that it wasn't Debs."[6] Debs's interest in learning also led him to help found a weekly debating society in Terre Haute known as the Occidental Literary Club. The fact that this organization sponsored lectures by prominent men had important results for the future Socialist leader. One of the speakers was the famous agnostic orator Robert G. Ingersoll who impressed Debs greatly and who must be considered among the important influences of his life. The club also sponsored several appearances by James Whitcomb Riley who became a close friend of Debs.

Debs's association with politics began in 1879 when his popularity in Terre Haute won him election to the position of city clerk, for which he ran on the Democratic ticket. He was reelected in 1881; and, after serving the second term, he made a successful campaign for the state legislature where he took his seat, again as a Democrat, in 1885. His campaign was motivated by a desire to help pass new laws to protect workers, but he had little success as a legislator. His attempt to push through a bill requiring railroads to pay employees for injuries suffered on the job was frustrated; and, in general, his experience in the legislature was unsuccessful. Discouraged, he declined to run for reelection; and the man who was to seek the presidency of the United States in no fewer than five campaigns declared that he would never again stand for public office.

During these years in city and state government, Debs was also active in the Brotherhood of Locomotive Firemen. From secretary of the Terre Haute lodge he rose to become assistant editor of the *Locomotive Firemen's Magazine*, in 1878, and, two years later, he became editor of the magazine as well as secretary-treasurer of the Brotherhood. As a high official of the union, his task was a formidable one, for the fortunes of the organization had sagged so low that most of the delegates at the national convention of 1880 were ready to give up. Debs, who wouldn't let them do so, promised to remove the debt that plagued the Brotherhood and convinced the delegates that they should keep the organization in existence for at least another year. Debs and the other officers of the Brotherhood then went to work to make good their promises, and they succeeded. Membership increased, the debt was eliminated, and the *Locomotive Firemen's Magazine* came to be read outside the Brotherhood as well as within it. Debs was well on his way toward making a reputation as a foremost labor leader.

Tall and handsome, genial and charming, with growing prestige both in politics and in the labor movement, Debs was attractive to the girls of Terre Haute. But not until 1885, when he was nearing the age of thirty, did he marry Kate Metzel. The marriage was childless, and Kate had to endure many lonely nights, for, both as labor organizer and Socialist leader, Debs spent much of his time away from home. Not an outgoing person, his wife became preoccupied with books and housework; and her longing for a home of her own led the Debs to build the large house on North Eighth Street, then one of the wealthiest sections of Terre Haute. Imposing in its day, the house is now dwarfed by the buildings of Indiana State University; but Debs's home is maintained essentially as it was when he lived there by the Eugene V. Debs Foundation.

II   *Early Ideas*

For a man who was the principal actor in one of the most famous labor struggles in American history, the Pullman Strike of 1894, as well as in countless other labor disputes, it is most interesting to read some of Debs's early statements on the subject of strikes and boycotts. As a fledgling labor-union official, he was by no means wholeheartedly devoted to the use of such means by the worker. In the December, 1883, issue of the *Locomotive Firemen's Magazine*, he wrote that "we do not believe in violence and strikes as means by which wages are to be regulated, but that all differences must be settled by mutual understanding arrived at by calm reasoning."[7] In the following year, he again stated that "the best for locomotive firemen is not to be found within the domain of STRIKES. A strike means war. The shibboleth motto of locomotive firemen is peace."[8] Debs also had some harsh words for the boycott during the 1880's, for he called it "a terrible weapon, to be used *only* when a terrible wrong exists." He felt that the boycott should never have been imported from Ireland because conditions in the United States did not warrant its use. Boycotting in his country, Debs insisted, has always been "a mistake, a stupid error, a total misapprehension of conditions, situation, institutions and rights." If it were ever used, the boycott was to be "adopted when all else has failed and when the wrongs complained of touch the very marrow of existence."[9]

Debs is not renowned for forecasting the future with great accuracy, and one of his grosser failures was his prediction that strikes would decline in number. The workers, he believed, would master their problems "by logic and law, and by the intelligent use of the ballot. . . ."[10] They would "seek assiduously for means of bettering their condition, apart from strikes and the boycott. They will discard anarchy and anarchists, violence by whatever name it is known, or by whatever method it may seek to gain its ends. . . ."[11] By 1887, Debs still declared that the *Locomotive Firemen's Magazine* was opposed to strikes, but his position seemed to be weakening. "We by no means are to be understood as favoring strikes, except as the last resort," he wrote.[12]

The disastrous Chicago, Burlington and Quincy strike of 1888, in which the firemen participated, apparently was the last straw which changed Debs's attitude toward strikes. There was no question about the justice of this strike, he declared in the *Locomotive Firemen's Magazine*.[13] And, as for the strike in general, it was "the weapon of the oppressed, of men capable of appreciating justice and having the courage to resist wrong and contend for principle."[14] Although he still maintained that he was opposed to the strike "as an original proposition," he believed that "there are times when every expedient to obtain justice has failed that the strike is absolutely justifiable."[15] Thus, during the 1880's, Debs's attitude toward strikes changed from opposition to a somewhat reluctant acceptance when other measures had failed.

Debs was also concerned during this period with the question of joint union activity by all railroad workers. But here, too, a change in his thinking can be detected; he began by making cautious statements about the brotherhoods working together, and he ended by championing the idea of one big union to which all railroad men would belong. His experience as a union official had convinced him that all railroad employees, regardless of their particular jobs, had mutual interests and should band together to achieve the goals they sought. From the mid-1880's he worked to put across this idea. In 1886, in a *Locomotive Firemen's Magazine* editorial entitled "Unity of Action among Locomotive Enginemen," Debs indicated that success in adjusting labor disputes "is certain when the engineer and fireman stand together side by side and shoulder to shoulder in every conflict involving their respective or their mutual rights. . . . They have got to be united and act together, and hence it follows that the two Brotherhoods should cultivate friendship, harmony and a unity of purpose and action. . . ."[16]

But it was necessary to proceed cautiously. There was the fear that unity might go too far, and the dreaded possibility seemed to be "amalgamation." At least Debs seemed to feel that it was necessary to say that loss of individual identity for the brotherhoods was not likely to be the result of working together. In the same 1886 editorial he continued:

We confess to having no patience with those who will affect to fear that friendship will breed amalgamation. . . . We are not afraid to trust these men. We have faith in their intelligence and their manhood, and we know that they are fully capable of preserving the equilibrium of their respective Brotherhoods and perpetuating them in all their usefulness and dignity and that in doing so they require no iron-clad rules of conduct to prevent them from becoming too intimate with each other.[17]

In the same issue of the *Locomotive Firemen's Magazine*, Debs denied a rumor that the Brotherhood of Locomotive Firemen and the Knights of Labor were discussing a merger, and he made it clear that such a possibility was not desirable. "While we desire the friendship and good will of all organizations with laudable ambitions," he wrote, "we are unalterably opposed to any scheme looking to the consolidation of our Order with any other of the numerous labor organizations."[18] Later that year, at its thirteenth annual convention, the Brotherhood of Locomotive Firemen went on record as being opposed to amalgamation with any other organization and instructed the editor of the magazine to make this clear to the public. "The Brotherhood of Locomotive Firemen takes no stock in amalgamation," Debs wrote in implementing the instructions of the convention. "It does not propose to unite, to coalesce with any other organization."[19]

Although amalgamation was banned, federation was something else again. Early in 1887, Debs, once again making use of the editorial page of the *Locomotive Firemen's Magazine*, declared that, "if labor is ever to reach the goal of equality with capital, in shaping policies, in the assertion of prerogatives, it will have to federate."[20] But a year later he seems to have retreated from this view, for "fraternal unity" took the place of federation. He was pleased to see good relationships existing among the various railroad organizations; he had been working for fraternal unity. This brotherly unity, he was careful to state, "does not mean federation, but fraternity; it means an advance on parallel lines to higher planes; it means that these Brotherhoods while one as the sea, one in the great fundamental purpose of improving conditions, in elevating character, are separate as the waves moving in grand procession toward separate and distinct goals." He promised that the *Locomotive Firemen's Magazine* would work for the "fullest realization" of fraternal unity as it had in the past.[21]

This brief deviation from the goal of federation, if it was that, did not last long. The unsuccessful Chicago, Burlington and Quincy strike of 1888, which contributed greatly to his change of attitude toward strikes, also convinced Debs that federation was necessary. In "Federation, the Lesson of the Great Strike," which appeared in the April, 1888, issue of the *Locomotive Firemen's Magazine*, Debs declared: "If corporations and the press confederate to overwhelm workingmen when they demand redress for grievances, they too must federate to enforce their rights which corporations deny them when demands are made in a becoming manner." Federation, he believed, would bring an end to strikes because a strike would bring all activities on the struck railroad to an immediate halt. "Instead of a strike there would be arbitration, a patient consideration of grievances when presented, and a prompt application of remedies when found."[22]

During the next four years Debs was involved in his efforts to bring about federation. In June, 1888, he called upon all labor organizations in the United States to consider federation. "United for mutual protection, workingmen of America would be invincible," Debs declared. "Once federated in the interest of right and justice, they would exert a moral power which would bear down all opposition. In that event, strikes would disappear and peace and prosperity would reign supreme." Clearly, Debs was in danger of being carried away with his grandiose ideas, a quality that never left him even when the ideas themselves changed. But, at the same time that he made this proposal, Debs again found it necessary to ward off the charge of "amalgamation." "It must not be understood that in advocating federation we favor the abandonment of separate and distinct organizations," he wrote. "We do not favor amalgamation."[23]

Federation provided the dominant theme of Debs's writing during this period, and for a time his efforts seemed about to bear fruit. In September, 1888, the Brotherhood of Locomotive Firemen endorsed federation at their convention, and, less than a year later, the representatives of the Firemen, Brakemen and Switchmen met to organize the Supreme Council of the United Orders of Railway Employees.[24] For a while the new federation was successful; Debs's dream seemed to have been realized; but a conflict developed within the organization and it was dissolved in 1892. Debs's hopes of federation dissolved with it.

Even before this blow Debs had determined to leave the Brotherhood for a variety of reasons. He had worked hard and seen the organization grow into a large and stable union. He felt that he had contributed about all he could, and he looked to other outlets for his abilities such as editing a paper concerned with all of labor. In addition, the growth of the Brotherhood had forced him to devote much of his time to tedious routine work. Finally, he wished to please Kate who was disturbed because of her enforced loneliness and because of her concern for his health. As a result of these factors, he announced in 1891 his intention to resign from his offices in the Brotherhood. The collapse of the Supreme Council of the United Orders of Railway Employees the following year convinced him that his dream of a federation of all railroad employees could not be achieved within the existing system of craft unionism, and he told his belief to the delegates at the 1892 Firemen's convention. But they, reluctant to let him go, refused to accept his resignation. Ultimately, it was agreed that he would remain as editor, which he did until 1894, but that he would resign as secretary-treasurer.

III   *The American Railway Union and the Pullman Strike*

Although Debs had abandoned his plans to bring about a federation of the existing Brotherhoods, his dream about combining all railroad employees in one union was not forgotten; and his energies were soon absorbed in planning a new labor organization which came into being in 1893. Membership in this American Railway Union was open to all white workers who labored in whatever capacity for a railroad, with the exception of managerial employees. Debs was made president of the union; and, with considerable confidence in the success of the venture, he set about recruiting members. His organizing trips kept him busy, but his task was not a very arduous one, for the railroaders were enthusiastic and joined the American Railway Union (ARU) in large numbers during late 1893 and early 1894. An important test of the new organization's strength came in the spring of 1894 when a decrease in wages on James J. Hill's Great Northern Railroad led to a strike. In spite of Hill's order to fire all workers who were sympathetic to the ARU, the Great Northern was effectively closed, and Hill ultimately agreed to arbitration of the union's demands. The award resulted in the strikers' winning nearly all of their demands—a great victory and morale booster for Debs and his new union.

Yet, within a few short months, the organization which had begun so auspiciously would be all but destroyed. The great Pullman Strike of 1894 not only shattered the hopes of the ARU; it was one of the important turning points in Debs's life. The employees of the Pullman Palace Car Company were particularly hard hit by the depression that wracked the United States in the mid-1890's. They were faced not only with wage cuts, layoffs, and poor working conditions, but with conditions in the company town of Pullman, Illinois, that were something less than desirable. The town was ruled in an arbitrary manner by the company, which resulted in considerable hardship for the residents. Rents were generally higher than elsewhere in the Chicago area and, to compound difficulties, the company refused to decrease rents when wages were reduced.

Even before the 1890's depression, the reputation of Pullman was odious in labor circles. In the January, 1887, issue of the *Locomotive Firemen's Magazine*, Debs himself, obviously unaware that within a decade his name and Pullman's would be inextricably linked, had attacked the sleeping-car manufacturer in an editorial. "The term 'Pullman,' " he wrote, "has become at last the synonym of almost anything odious that heartless, crushing, degrading monopoly suggests to the minds of honorable men. . . ." The name suggests great wealth, "cringing, fawning lickspittles", autocratic rule, and underpaid workers. "It is such vindictive practices," Debs continued, interestingly enough in view of his later career, "that breed the unrest and vindictive spirit abroad in the lands that furnish anarchists and socialists with the raw material for their diatribes against law and social order. . . ."[25]

Such conditions were obviously compounded by the bad times in the 1890's. In May, 1894, a committee of workers complained to management about wages and working conditions; and, dissatisfied with the equivocal manner in which they were received, they decided to strike. Many of the workers were members of the ARU, eligible for membership because the Pullman Company operated a few miles of track. Although the strike was not authorized by the ARU, Debs went to Pullman to discover what was going on.

The national convention of the American Railway Union was held in Chicago in June, and whether or not to support the Pullman Strike was one of the important considerations confronting the delegates. Most were in favor of doing so by means of a boycott of Pullman Palace cars; but Debs, although unquestionably sympathetic with the strikers, warned against precipitate action. He counselled a go-slow policy for a number of reasons, and the most important reason was probably his fear that the ARU was not prepared to engage in such an action.

Because the union was young, because most of its members were inexperienced, and because it had no strike funds, its chances of losing a strike against the powerful Pullman Company were great. At Debs's suggestion, a committee was appointed to discuss the strike with representatives of the company; but the move was futile. When another committee had met with similar results, Debs could no longer restrain the delegates; and the convention voted unanimously to begin the boycott on June 26. ARU switchmen were instructed not to switch Pullman Palace cars; and, if they lost their jobs as a result, all other ARU members on the offending railroad were to strike. Thus the stage was set—for disaster.

But the disaster for the strikers was not obvious from the beginning. More than one hundred thousand men were on strike, and there was very little regular railway service west of Chicago. Much to Debs's delight, a minimum of violence occurred. By July 1, the future looked bright for the strikers. However, a formidable array of foes was opposed to the young and inexperienced ARU. The railroads were determined not only to break the strike but to destroy the union, and they had powerful assets to back them up. The most potent of these resources was the federal government; for, more than any other factor, the support of the government ultimately crushed the Pullman Strike and destroyed Debs's union.

The railroads' closest ally in the government was Attorney General Richard Olney who, as a lawyer in private life, had represented railroads and had served on the boards of directors of several. At the suggestion of the General Managers Association, an organization which represented the railroads terminating or centering in Chicago, one of Olney's first moves was to appoint Edwin Walker as a special federal attorney to deal with the strike. The fact that Walker was a lawyer for one of the railroads involved in the strike suggests where his sympathies lay.

As if the hostility of the attorney general were not enough, Debs and his union received a second blow on July 2 when an injunction was issued by the Federal Court in Chicago forbidding the strike leaders to assist the boycott in any way. Faced wtth a decision to risk jail or see the strike end, to see the union crushed, and to have thousands of blacklisted railroaders out of work, Debs and the other union officers decided to defy the injunction and continued to direct the strike. For this decision, they would spend several months in jail.

But Olney was not satisfied that the federal government had done enough to break the strike; and in spite of the opposition of Governor Altgeld who insisted that state and local forces could handle the situation, President Cleveland sent federal troops into Chicago on July 4. Their mission was to protect federal property (although it was not apparent that federal property was threatened), prevent obstruction of the mail (although none was accumulating in Chicago), prevent interference with interstate commerce (although the only major interference with interstate commerce was the refusal of strikers to move Pullman cars), and enforce the decrees of the federal Court, the injunction against the strike leaders. There seems to be little question about the fact that the troops were not needed in Chicago; but since they were there, their presence spelled the doom of both the strike and the American Railway Union.

Before the arrival of the troops, hundreds of special deputy federal marshals had been recruited to help preserve order. Due to the temporary nature of the jobs, it was not to be expected that the best people would take them; and their ranks included labor spies, strikebreakers, thugs, and drunkards. In general, they did little good and a great deal of harm. Some of them caused unnecessary trouble, and the police superintendent thought that they were only in the way. What Attorney General Olney expected from these deputy marshals is difficult to say; perhaps as one historian suggests, he believed their inadequacy would demonstrate the need for federal troops.[26]

Debs was determined from the first to avoid violence, and there had been very little until the troops arrived. The American Railway Union leader was afraid that the presence of the troops would provoke it, and his fears seem to have been correct since, soon after the troops moved into Chicago, violence began and continued for several days. When riotous crowds gathered and clashed with soldiers several deaths and many injuries occurred; and hundreds of boxcars were burned, and switches were smashed. Exactly who was responsible has never been determined, but, since Debs labored diligently to keep his ARU men away from the trouble areas, it is unlikely that many of them were involved in the disorders. Certainly, violence worked in the interests of the railroads, not the strikers, for it tended to turn public opinion against the strike and the union.

There was little hope for the strike after the intervention of federal troops. Furthermore, Debs and other leaders of the ARU were arrested and charged with conspiracy to obstruct a mail train, and for violation of the federal injunction which forbade them to assist the boycott. The trial on the first charge ended when a juror became ill, and the case was never reopened. But, for contempt, Debs received a sentence of six months, the other ARU leaders three months, in jail. An appeal to the United States Supreme Court ended unfavorably, and Debs was forced to serve his six months at the McHenry County Jail in Woodstock, Illinois, and to leave behind him a shattered American Railway Union and more shattered dreams. But his imprisonment in 1895 marked the end of only one phase in Debs's career. He was only forty years of age, and a long and vigorous life lay before him.

CHAPTER 2

The Making of a Socialist

D EBS'S experience at Woodstock was much more pleasant than one might expect jail life to be. The jail was in the home of the sheriff, and the American Railway Union prisoners ate good food at the sheriff's table. Debs spent much of his time studying, editing the American Railway Union's *Railway Times*, and writing a weekly article for the Chicago *Evening Press*. He also had to cope with hundreds of letters a day as well as a large number of visitors. Clearly, incarceration did not halt the employment of Debs's boundless energy.

I *The Conversion*

Although everyone knows when Debs announced his conversion to Socialism, one finds it a more difficult matter to state with accuracy when Socialist ideas began to make a significant impact on him. It is obviously much too simple to say that his conversion occurred on the day that he announced it, for such fundamental changes in thought occur gradually over an extended period of time. Although he later stated that before the Pullman Strike he knew very little about Socialism and was not impressed by what he did know,[1] one can detect tendencies in his early life that facilitated his later acceptance of the Socialist doctrine. For example, his childhood exposure to writers who championed the cause of the common man must certainly have had an effect on him. His ardent support of the worker during his years as a labor-union official and his egalitarian attitudes that were frequently expressed in the *Locomotive Firemen's Magazine* editorials suggest a person who was not far removed from a Socialist outlook on life. In 1884, he condemned the massing of great wealth in the hands of one man as dangerous to the commercial interests of the country and to the liberty of the people. "To take a man's money out of his pocket is larceny," he wrote, "to

29

form a corner in wheat or stocks and thereby rob your neighbor of his fortune is business. . . . The remedy for these great wrongs must be soon found and applied." Although Socialism might have been recommended as the remedy, he did not suggest it in 1884; but he did state that "it should be made impossible for one man or a few men to control the property and happiness of thousands of their fellow creatures."[2] Although Debs's formal acceptance of Socialism was not to come for a dozen years, his conversion was obviously not a difficult one.

Without question, the Pullman Strike was a crucial event in Debs's conversion to Socialism. In 1903, he wrote of his "blissful ignorance" of Socialism before the strike and of his "utter failure to grasp the significance, scope and character of the Socialist movement. From crown to foot soles I was a 'pure and simple' trade unionist. . . ." He had had a "hazy conception" that Socialism "was akin to anarchy and that it was not of sufficient importance to merit serious attention." But, after the Pullman Strike, he continued, "I realized that Socialism had been thrust upon me at the point of a capitalist bayonet. . . ."[3] In another account of his conversion, he stated that, during the strike, "there was delivered, from wholly unexpected quarters, a swift succession of blows that blinded me for an instant and then opened wide my eyes—and in the gleam of every bayonet and the flash of every rifle *the class struggle was revealed*. This was my first practical lesson in Socialism, though wholly unaware that it was called by that name."[4]

In attempting to determine when Debs became converted to Socialism, his testimony before the presidential commission investigating the Pullman Strike is interesting and informative. In the first place, it must be noted that this testimony was given in August, 1894, immediately after the strike and before Debs served his term in jail. He made it clear that he favored government ownership of the railroads, but he went beyond this concept to advocate abolishing the entire wage system. In its place he called for a cooperative commonwealth, but he denied that he was a Socialist. "There is a wide difference in the interpretation or definition of the term," he said:

I believe in a cooperative commonwealth upon the principles laid down by Laurence Gronlund. You may have read his works. I believe that is the rational solution of the whole question. We recognize the main features of

State socialism. I can say in relation to the wage system that in my judgment—I am studying this question and I want much more light than I have got; I am in need of much more, and speak for nobody but myself—but I am impressed with the conviction that the social and industrial conditions will grow worse instead of better, so long as the wage system remains in vogue.[5]

This passage might very well be cited as evidence that Debs was somewhat unsympathetic to Socialism in 1894. After all, he stated flatly that he did not call himself a Socialist. But the opposite is closer to the truth. For he made it quite clear that he was opposed to the wage system and that he supported the views of Laurence Gronlund. The puzzling thing here is how Debs could say that he was not a Socialist but that he supported Gronlund. Gronlund's *Cooperative Commonwealth*, which had for its subtitle, *An Exposition of Modern Socialism*, was nothing more than a popularization of Marxism. Although ambiguities in the author's treatment of the class-struggle doctrine somewhat diluted the original Marxism, there is no question about this being a Marxist book.[6] Thus, when Debs said that he was a follower of Gronlund in 1894, he seemed to be saying that he was a Socialist. At the very least, one can conclude that he was giving Socialism serious attention at this time.

Although the Pullman Strike was obviously of great significance, Debs believed that it was at Woodstock "that Socialism gradually laid hold of me in its own irresistible fashion." He was inundated with Socialist writings during his six-month incarceration, and those by Edward Bellamy, Robert Blatchford, and Laurence Gronlund especially appealed to him. But he was particularly impressed by the Marxist Karl Kautsky whose writings he found "so clear and conclusive that I readily grasped, not merely his argument, but also caught the spirit of his Socialist utterance. . . ." Debs was visited at Woodstock by the Milwaukee Socialist, Victor Berger, who brought him a copy of Marx's *Das Kapital* and who "delivered the first impassioned message of Socialism I had ever heard—the very first to set the 'wires humming in my system.' "[7]

Hitting Debs at a time when he was basking in bitterness over his crushing defeat in Chicago, Woodstock was undoubtedly a key factor in Debs's conversion. But this factor was not the deciding one, for he did not announce his support of Socialism until more than a year after his release from jail. Following a triumphant welcome back to freedom by an estimated one hundred thousand well-wishers in Chicago, Debs turned his attention to the badly mauled American Railway Union. The railroads were relentless in their determination to destroy the union, and they were not satisfied with the crippling of the organization that the Pullman Strike had brought about. American Railway Union members were blacklisted and found it very difficult to get jobs. There was also the matter of a $30,000 debt at a time when dues were decreasing. Debs, in an effort to bring some money into the empty coffers, as well as to revive the union, went on a lecture tour.

Politically, Debs was in a transition period. Whatever sympathies he had once had for the Democratic party had been destroyed by the action of President Cleveland during the strike. For a man of Debs's outlook, abandoning the Democrats certainly did not mean joining the Republicans; and, inasmuch as he was not quite ready to call himself a Socialist, he was left only with the Populist party. Thus for a brief time, until the election of 1896, he supported the Populists and almost became their presidential candidate. There was support for him, but he requested those who backed his candidacy not to nominate him because, according to Ray Ginger, "his thinking was changing rapidly on basic questions of philosophy and strategy. He hesitated to identify himself completely with a capitalist reform party like the Populists."[8] But, since he wanted the People's Party to win in 1896, he gave many speeches in support of it.

There is little doubt that Debs had been moving rapidly toward Socialism while he officially supported Populism. Many of the statements that he made immediately before, during, and after his imprisonment suggest a mind that is very close to accepting Socialist theory. The Populist concern with the plight of the farmer and the free-silver issue, which was so important in the 1896 campaign, are not the main emphases in Debs's writings of this period. His concern is for the worker, and his rage is directed against the wage system and the capitalists behind it. "As long as workingmen vote the same ticket their masters vote they must expect to be doomed to slavery," he wrote in January, 1895. "When will workingmen have the good sense to follow the example of capitalists and vote together and vote *their interests?* . . . Nothing less than the complete overthrow of the grinding, degrading, pauperizing conspiracy against wageworkers will answer the demand. . . . Every man is entitled to *all* he produces with his brain and hands. The night of wage-competition is dark, but the dawn of co-operation is near at hand."[9] And again, later in the same year, he declared that "I am doing what little I can to emancipate my countrymen from degrading conditions. I realize that this can only be done by total abolishment of the wage system and the introduction of that infinitely more rational, just and humane system which contemplates the cooperation of all for the good of all."[10]

In November, 1895, on the day of his release from the Woodstock jail and after his arrival in Chicago to the happy shouts and screams of a hundred thousand well-wishers, Debs spoke about the subject of liberty to his admirers. "If liberty is ostracized and exiled," he said, using some of his most vivid imagery,

man is a slave, and the world rolls in space and whirls around the sun a gilded prison, a doomed dungeon, and though painted in all the enchanting hues that infinite art could command, it must still stand forth a blotch amidst the shining spheres of the sidereal heavens, and those who cull from the vocabularies of nations, living or dead, their flashing phrases with which to apostrophize Liberty, are engaged in perpetuating the most stupendous delusion the ages have known. Strike down liberty, no matter by what subtle and infernal art the deed is done, the spinal cord of humanity is sundered and the world is paralyzed by the indescribable crime.

But Debs had great faith in the power of the ballot which, he declared,

can make and unmake presidents and congresses and courts. It can abolish unjust laws and consign to eternal odium and oblivion unjust judges, strip from them their robes and gowns and send them forth unclean as lepers to bear the burden of merited obloquy as Cain with the mark of a murderer. It can sweep away trusts, syndicates, corporations, monopolies, and every other abnormal development of the money power designed to abridge the liberties of workingmen and enslave them by the degradation incident to poverty and enforced idleness, as cyclones scatter the leaves of the forest. The ballot can do all this and more. It can give our civilization its crowning glory—the co-operative commonwealth.[11]

If this speech does not contain good Socialist rhetoric, it is difficult to distinguish the real product. Of course, one could argue that a Populist who rejected Socialism completely might have uttered most of these statements, but such things as the focus on the plight

of the laborer rather than on that of the farmer, the demand for
abolition of the wage system, and the call for the cooperative
commonwealth which indicates the influence of Laurence Gronlund
suggest that, if Debs had not embraced Socialism over a year before
he publicly announced it, he had not far to go.

In spite of Debs's tendency toward Socialism, there is no question
about the fact that his plea for the intelligent use of the ballot in 1895
and 1896 meant that it should be used to support the Populist party
for which he seemed to have great hope. "This party," he wrote
from jail in August, 1895, "has become a standing menace to
plutocracy" because "It confronts and denounces its schemes
everywhere. . . . If it fulfills its mission, it will hold the balance of
power in the next congress and will dictate legislation. If not strong
enough to enact its reform measures into laws, it will be strong
enough to arrest infamous legislation by either of the two old parties. Standing by the right, yielding never a jot or tittle of its reform
principles, the people will indorse its fealty to the welfare of the
nation and with the new century it will come into possession of the
government." Debs was convinced that the Populist vote would
increase substantially in 1896 and that the party would ride to an
overwhelming victory in 1900.[12]

The defeat of William J. Bryan and the Populist cause in the
election of 1896, which effectively killed Debs's hopes for a re-
sounding victory in 1900, were all that he needed to announce his
conversion to Socialism, and he made such an announcement on
January 1, 1897. In his statement he suggested a somewhat
lukewarm attachment to Populism during the campaign. He supported Bryan and the Populist platform "not because I regarded the
free coinage of silver as a panacea for our national ills, for I neither
affirmed nor advocated such a principle, but because I believed that
the triumph of Mr. Bryan and free silver would blunt the fangs of
the money power. . . ." He saw the free-silver issue as a rallying
cry, as a common ground upon which the common people could
unite against the money power which had all but ruined the country. Once united, he declared, the common people "could press
forward in a solid phalanx in the crusade against social and industrial
slavery, nor halt in the advancing columns until the whole capitalistic system is abolished and the co-operative commonwealth has
become an established fact." Thus it would seem that, even in his
support of Populism, Debs had Socialist ends in mind.

The election, he continued, "has convinced every intelligent wageworker that in politics, per se, there is no hope of emancipation from the degrading curse of wage slavery." The ballot, in which he had placed so much faith during the campaign, "has been beaten to the earth by boodle wrung from unrequited toil, and as a weapon cannot be relied upon to execute the will of the people while they are in industrial bondage. An industrial slave cannot be expected to cast an independent ballot." That his conversion to Socialism was no sudden occurrence is also made apparent by his statement that "I have long since given expression to my socialistic convictions; they have grown with my growth and I am more strongly impressed with them at this hour than ever before since first I began the painful study of the progress and poverty of the race." The competitive system is cannibalistic, with men set one against another, he declared; and he pledged himself to its overthrow. "The issue is, Socialism vs. Capitalism. I am for Socialism because I am for humanity. We have been cursed with the reign of gold long enough. Money constitutes no proper basis of civilization. The time has come to regenerate society—we are on the eve of a universal change."[13] Strong words—but, except for the substitution of "socialism" for "Populism," there is no great change in the statements that Debs had been making since the Pullman strike.

II *A Flirtation with Communitarianism*

Debs's initial experience with Socialism was with the communitarian rather than with the Marxian variety. Much to the chagrin of Marxists, who had been initially delighted when Debs embraced Socialism, he became associated with the Brotherhood of the Cooperative Commonwealth. This organization, founded in 1895, had three goals in mind: to spread the principles of Socialism among the American people; to bring about the union of all co-operationists in the country into one body; and, most importantly, to colonize a Western state with enough sympathizers to take over the state government and establish a Socialist commonwealth.[14]

Early in 1897, Debs joined the Brotherhood as a national organizer, but his membership in the organization was brief. He was attracted to it mainly because of the colonization scheme which he saw as providing a refuge for the host of American Railway Union members who had been blacklisted as a result of the Pullman strike. But it was not long before ineffective leadership of the Brotherhood convinced him that little would be accomplished for his union men in the immediate future, and he soon abandoned the organization. He did not leave behind the colonization idea, however, for he continued to regard it as a solution to the problems of many American Railway Union men. Realizing that the American Railway Union could no longer continue effectively as a labor union, he proposed to convert it into a colonization organization; and he issued a call for a special convention to meet in Chicago on June 15, 1897.[15]

No amount of defeat—and Debs had more than his share during his lifetime—seemed to prevent him from expecting great things of the future. As he did with all the projects that he became involved in, he supported the colonization plan with great zest and high hopes. In an issue of *The Western Miner* that appeared just three days before the American Railway Union convention met, Debs explained in some detail the program that he would put before the delegates. "The movement to be launched at Chicago," he wrote, "contemplates the unification of all workers, organized and unorganized, and all others, regardless of sex or color, who favor a change in our social and industrial affairs and believe it can be brought about only by a complete change of our social and industrial system." The organization would have a brief constitution and a declaration of principles. Organizers would be sent out to establish branches in every state. That the members be well-informed he felt was of the utmost importance for "there is nothing weaker than organized ignorance." Thus "powerful educational influences would be set in operation" immediately, and each member would receive a copy of the organization's official paper which would be "the very best paper of the kind issued." A book and pamphlet department was to be established "and every good work and treatise upon economics and kindred subjects can be here obtained at actual cost. A modern and well equipped printing plant will be established and economic literature will be produced in cheap editions and large quantities, which will be freely distributed, especially among the poor who lack the means to buy."

The article showed that Debs had given considerable thought to the new venture and had worked out many details. Oddly enough, in view of his general distaste for the military, he seemed to envisage a semimilitary type of organization, at least in its embryo stages: "The first of these pioneers will, no doubt, be required to march, but this will be done under perfect order and discipline. First of all, each applicant for enlistment must be examined and accepted by the recruiting officers. Only such will be accepted as comprehend fully the nature of the undertaking, the purpose sought to be accomplished and whose hearts are thoroughly in the movement. Respect for discipline and obedience to regulations will be exacted." The first colonists would probably be unmarried men or men without families, Debs declared, and they might have to expect to undergo "privations." Yet fundamental respect for mankind convinced him that they would meet the test. "They will be men of much fibre," he wrote, "and the conviction that they are the progenitors of a new humanity will burn and glow in their breasts with such intensity, that come what may, they will have the courage and fidelity to stand and withstand until success is achieved."

The special dedication required of the members would not make them difficult to find, Debs believed; he expected that the organization would soon number one hundred thousand and $25,000 a month would be rolling into the treasury. "With this amount," he continued, "the pioneers can be provided for, lands can be secured, agricultural machinery purchased, factories erected and such productive enterprises established as the state may be best adapted to. All of this will be well under way prior to the next following state election." At that time a slate of Socialists would be run for state offices; and, after the victory (which went without saying), a new constitution "compatible with the co-operative commonwealth" would be put into operation. "The public will acquire ownership and control of all the means of production and distribution, and there will be one state beneath the American flag in which a man, willing to work, will be able to secure employment. . . ." Every worker "will secure the full product of his toil," but there would be no "idlers," Debs insisted in fine puritanical fashion. "They who will not work may not eat."

Not only did the American Railway Union leader have high hopes for the success of his project, but he was certain that the scheme would soon spread and envelop the country. "In the national campaign of 1900," he wrote, "the new movement will be a factor in the election. Its political principles will be those of the Socialist Labor party and its political battles will, doubtless, be fought under the banner of that party." He predicted that two million votes would be polled in 1900, and in 1904 the movement would carry the country, whereupon great things would happen: "Gaunt famine and the spectre of failure will be remembered only as hideous nightmares. Humanity will then be emancipated from the horrible thraldoms which a soulless money oligarchy has forced upon it, and a free and happy people will march forward with majestic strides toward a diviner civilization."[16]

Debs took his grandiose scheme to the sparsely attended American Railway Union convention on June 15, 1897, and he induced the delegates to dissolve the Union and to establish in its place the Social Democracy of America. In line with Debs's ideas, the new organization's Declaration of Principles stated that "one of the states of the Union, to be hereafter determined, shall be selected for the concentration of our supporters and the introduction of co-operative industry and then gradually extending the sphere of our operations until the National Co-operative Commonwealth shall be established." The constitution of the Social Democracy of America provided for local branches which would be limited to five hundred members each and for state unions made up of one representative from each local branch. The legislative functions of the organization were to be carried out by a National Council which was to consist of one representative from each state and territory while an Executive Board was given general supervisory power. Debs was elected chairman of the Executive Board.

Due to the efforts of Victor Berger and other politically inclined Socialists who were appalled at Debs's infatuation with the colonization scheme, the Social Democracy of America also adopted a political program. A list of immediate demands was compiled that included a call for public ownership of all industries controlled by monopolies, trusts, and combines; of transportation and communication facilities; and of mines, oil wells, and mineral deposits. It also called for shorter working hours, for a public works program for the unemployed, for a postal savings bank; for initiative, referendum, and recall; and for proportional representation.[17]

From the beginning, a wide divergence existed between those who emphasized the political aspects of the Social Democracy and those whose main interest was colonization. Oddly enough, in view of the great stress Debs had placed on the colonization plan, he stated soon after the convention that the purpose of the organization was primarily political and that the colonization scheme had been overemphasized. The controversy continued for a year, and it came to a head at the second national convention of the Social Democracy in June, 1898. A bitter clash between the two factions ended in a victory for the colonizationists and in a walkout by those who favored political action. Torn between the two factions, Debs equivocated. He gave a speech at the convention in which he sang the praises of colonization with his usual gusto: "Give me 10,000 men, aye 10,000 in a western state with access to the sources of production, and we will change the economic conditions, and we will convince the people of that state, win their hearts and their intelligence. We will lay hold upon the reins of government and plant the flag of Socialism upon the State House."[18] But after the split in the convention, Debs threw in his lot with the political actionists.

The split was fatal to the Social Democracy of America. Many local branches abandoned the organization to join the political actionists, and insufficient funds soon drove the Social Democracy newspaper, the *Social Democrat*, out of business. A colony was eventually settled in the State of Washington, but it did not last long enough to capture the state for Socialism.[19] At the end of the nineteenth century, the hope for Socialist victory lay in the development of a healthy and active political party rather than in communitarianism. At some point, Debs must have perceived this for, despite his vigorous championing of colonization and his obvious reluctance to abandon it, he chose the political road.

CHAPTER 3

A Socialist's Life

FOR the rest of his life, Eugene Debs carried the banner for a Socialist political party; and he labored vigorously to spread the Socialist gospel throughout the United States. Although he ran five times for the presidency, his goal was not really to win but to use the presidential campaign to educate the workingman in the evils of capitalism and in the virtues of Socialism. For his efforts, he was far from richly rewarded. Poor health dogged him and frequently prostrated him temporarily. He was, for a second time, forced to serve a term in prison. And he witnessed in his last years a Socialist decline rather than the glorious triumph he had anticipated ever since his conversion. But is it entirely accurate to say that Debs was not rewarded? For some, after all, the effort itself is a kind of reward. Would it not be a most satisfying experience if one could, in one's declining years, look back on a long life of struggle for a good cause to which one was passionately dedicated?

I *The Presidential Campaigns*

The political actionists who walked out of the Social Democracy convention in 1898 lost little time in establishing a new organization, the Social Democratic party. After Debs supported it and was elected to the Executive Board, he soon made a lecture tour to sing the praises of his new party; and the early success of the organization owed much to his efforts. He gave many speeches in Massachusetts prior to the elections of 1898 which saw two Social Democrats elected to the Massachusetts legislature from Haverhill and a third elected mayor of the city. When it came time to select a presidential candidate in 1900, Debs was the natural choice. He was reluctant to accept the nomination due to poor health and to his need to continue lecturing to pay off the American Railway Union debt; but, after considerable pleading by his supporters, he agreed to run.

40

In the campaign of 1900, Debs was also the choice for president of a group of Socialists who were not yet members of the Social Democratic party. During the previous year, a faction in the Socialist Labor party (led by Morris Hillquit) rebelled against the leadership of Daniel DeLeon and left the party. This group, known as "Kangaroos," suggested a union with the fledgling Social Democratic party, a proposal that met with a mixed response from that party. Many among the rank and file were in favor of uniting, but others were reluctant to join with men who had only recently been associated with DeLeon. Debs himself was torn; on the one hand, he favored unity; but he was plagued with doubt because of his dislike for DeLeon in particular and for the Socialist Labor party in general.

Kangaroo delegates were invited to attend the Social Democratic party convention in 1900; and, although a formal unity was not achieved, the former Socialist Labor party members agreed to support Debs for President. One of the Kangaroo leaders, Job Harriman, was nominated by both groups to be Debs's running mate. Debs conducted a strenuous campaign, and the vote of slightly under one hundred thousand that he received was disappointing to him. But anyone with the indomitable optimism of Debs could not easily be discouraged. "This will be one of the last convulsions of capitalism before the social revolution sweeps it out of existence," he declared. "The next four years will witness the development of socialism to continental power and proportions."[1]

Although Debs, as usual, exaggerated the future accomplishments of Socialism, the years following the campaign of 1900 were not uneventful for American Socialism and for Debs. In 1901, differences between the Social Democratic party and the Kangaroos were ironed out so that they, as well as a number of independent Socialists, were able to form the Socialist party of America. Debs's distaste for the kind of haggling that occurs at such gatherings kept him away from the convention that completed the merger. He claimed illness in the family but, as one historian of Socialism has stated, "sicknesses seemingly had a habit of coming to Debs or his family when unpleasantries at socialist gatherings threatened to develop."[2] As usual, however, he did not shrink from praising the virtues of Socialism on his lecture tours which, save for the always unprofitable Debs Publishing Company that he had established, were his sole source of income during these early years of the new century.

In 1904, Debs was again a reluctant candidate for President of the United States, and another exhausting campaign ended in a most satisfying result for the Socialists. Debs received more than four hundred thousand votes, four times the 1900 total. Clearly, Debs and his colleagues believed that the Socialist party was heading for victory in the not-too-distant future.

Thus Debs and the Socialist party approached the election of 1908 with great optimism. Between the elections, the organization had grown stronger, for the membership was double what it had been four years before. But Debs was in poor health because of rheumatism, lumbago, and headaches; and he had just completed an exhausting lecture tour. This ill health provided members of the party's right wing with some ammunition and, at the nominating convention, they placed in nomination the name of Algie M. Simons, former editor of the *International Socialist Review*. As usual, Debs's dislike of conventions kept him away, but a friend who was present had a letter from the Socialist leader which was read to the delegates. In it, Debs stated that his health was "about all that could be desired. So far as strength is concerned, I never had more to my credit, if as much." Although he did not want to run for or to hold an office, he expressed a desire to "make myself as big and as useful as I can, as much opposed to the enemy and as much loved by our comrades as any man in the ranks. You need have no fear that I shall shirk my part in the coming campaign. I shall be in condition, and I hope there will be no good ground for complaint when the fight is over."[3] The letter clinched his nomination, for an overwhelming majority of the votes went to Debs on the first ballot.

The campaign was as strenuous as usual. It was also colorful. An outstanding feature was the Red Special, a rented train that carried Debs and his entourage around the country, stopping at small towns as well as in large cities. It was greeted enthusiastically wherever it went, but the tour was particularly exhausting for Debs who had to greet party workers and supporters at every stop. Financing was always a problem and, at one point during the Red Special's Western tour, there was a danger that the train would be stranded on the West Coast. But emergency appeals for funds were answered with enough money to allow the Red Special to continue.

In view of the general enthusiasm that greeted Debs across the country and the vigor of the campaign, the results of the election of 1908 were particularly disappointing. While Debs predicted a million votes, and other Socialists had even higher hopes, he received only 420,793, a negligible increase over 1904. The cooperative commonwealth might be coming, but the pace at which it was moving was discouragingly slow. Badly in need of rest, Debs gave no lectures for almost a year after the election of 1908. Yet he could not be completely idle; and he spent much of his time in Girard, Kansas, writing for the Socialist weekly, *Appeal to Reason*. He had joined the staff in 1907. The respite from speaking helped him, so that he recovered rapidly and, by November, 1909, he was ready to return to the lecture platform.

This time the occasion was a tour to aid in the defense of Fred Warren, editor of the *Appeal*. Warren had been fined and sentenced to six months in jail because of some objectionable articles that had been published in the *Appeal* two years before. One, written by Debs, was concerned with the Haywood, Moyer, Pettibone case. In 1906, Big Bill Haywood, Charles Moyer, and George Pettibone were arrested and extradited from Colorado to Idaho for the murder of Frank Steunenberg, former governor of Idaho. The three were arrested on a Saturday night when the courts were closed, thus preventing them from seeking a stay of extradition; they were spirited across the state line in a special train and indicted for murder. Debs insisted that the men were innocent—that their indictment was really an attack on all of organized labor. The affair brought forth some of Debs's most violent statements, and one of his articles in which he denounced the extradition as illegal caused the government to move against the *Appeal*.[4]

Warren had penned the second troublesome article himself. In it, he told of a former governor of Kentucky, wanted for questioning in a murder case, who had gone to Indiana where the governor had refused to permit his extradition. Referring to the Moyer, Haywood, Pettibone case, Warren pointed out that while capitalist politicians were not extradited legally when they should have been, labor leaders were extradited illegally. Because of these articles, Warren was indicted and convicted for sending "scurrilous, defamatory and threatening" literature through the mails.

Fearing that indictments would be brought against other editors and that the very existence of the *Appeal* would be threatened, the verdict was appealed; and Debs went on his lecture tour to convince the public of Warren's innocence. Another year passed before a Federal Circuit Court upheld Warren's sentence, but this fact did not stop Debs. He again set out on a lecture tour, for he was determined to prevent the imprisonment of the *Appeal* editor. How much Debs's efforts had to do with it is difficult to say, but in February, 1911, President Taft reduced the sentence to a hundred-dollar fine—a fine, incidentally, which was never paid.

At the 1912 convention of the Socialist party, the right wing tried even harder than it had in 1908 to defeat the nominatiion of Debs. But the party members were unable to unite on one candidate, and the result was that Debs, although he himself preferred Fred Warren, again became the standard bearer. But the factional controversy did not end with the nomination. The right wing managed to secure the choice of a campaign manager whom Debs opposed, and a battle before the party's National Executive Committee ended in the defeat of Debs's attempt to oust him. The Socialist leader, who was bitter, later that year wrote privately that, although the right-wing leadership, which he referred to as the "machine," could not defeat his nomination, it did get control of his campaign, "and it is not an accident that since the machine has been set upon destroying me, or at least my influence, my campaigns have been managed by those who did all in their power to defeat my nomination."[5]

But, in spite of his problems, Debs conducted the usual, energetic campaign. Two of his opponents, Theodore Roosevelt and Woodrow Wilson, were running on liberal platforms and undoubtedly took many votes away from him. Yet, in spite of this handicap, 1912 turned out to be the most successful presidential campaign ever conducted by American Socialists. The final vote showed that 897,011 voters had cast their ballots for Debs. Even more significant was the fact that this figure constituted nearly six per cent of the total. Later Socialist campaigns would produce more votes for the candidates, but never again would an American Socialist receive such a high percentage of the total.

In the year following the election, Debs, nearing sixty, decided to retire and live on the income from his occasional writing. He resigned from the staff of the *Appeal to Reason*, abandoned the lecture circuit, and settled down in the comfort of his large Terre Haute home—for two months! When, in February, 1914, Frank O'Hare, editor of a Socialist monthly called the *National Rip-Saw*, asked him to join the staff as editorial writer and lecturer, Debs accepted. For a man of Debs's energy, retirement was a state of life most difficult to achieve.

II *World War I and Imprisonment*

As it was for much of the world, Debs's chief concern over the next few years was centered around the subject of war; and he began with a condemnation of the landing of American Marines at Vera Cruz, Mexico, in April, 1914. In response to the outbreak of war in Europe, he called for complete neutrality; and he worked diligently for peace on the lecture platform and in *Rip-Saw* editorials. In late 1915 and early 1916, he opposed the American preparedness movement and, as the United States approached involvement in the conflict in 1917, Debs called for a general strike as the response to an American declaration of war.

The only campaign between 1900 and 1920 in which Debs was not the presidential candidate of the Socialist party was the 1916 race. Since he was not well and since his wife wanted him to forego the strenuous campaign, Debs decided to step aside in favor of a younger candidate. Allan L. Benson, a journalist and Socialist propagandist, was nominated in his place. Although Benson was not a party leader, his writings had made him well known to the rank and file, and this factor was especially important in a year when the nomination was made by popular referendum instead of a party convention. But his campaign was not a successful one; he polled only 585,113 votes as compared to the nearly 900,000 that Debs had received in 1912.[6]

Although Debs refused the presidential candidacy, he was not inactive during the 1916 campaign. Indiana Socialists nominated him to be their candidate for Congress from his home district, and he accepted. Concentrating his attack on the war in Europe, he conducted his usual arduous campaign which received attention and support from Socialists all over the world. But, of course, he did not win; although he received more votes than the Democratic incumbent, the Republican candidate was the victor. " 'Blessed are they who expect nothing,' " Debs declared, " 'for they shall not be disappointed.' "[7]

The entry of the United States into World War I in April, 1917, caused a serious split in the Socialist party. Officially, the party declared itself in opposition to the war; but many members had different ideas. While they had been firmly opposed to American involvement in the conflict, now that the United States had become a belligerent nation, people such as Algie M. Simons, John Spargo,

Allan Benson, and William English Walling felt that the government should be supported. And they felt strongly enough about it to
resign from the Socialist party. Debs was greatly troubled by both
the American declaration of war and the split, for he did not like to
oppose his old friends who had left the party. Although he remained
unwaveringly opposed to the war, he seemed for a year after America's entry to be restrained—unsure of what course to follow. But, by
the middle of 1918, Debs, angered by the suppression of radicals by
the government and the jailing of some of his Socialist comrades,
decided to speak out vigorously against the war; and his lecturing,
which had largely ceased after the United States joined the conflict
in Europe, began again. His object was not only to bring about
opposition to the war but to taunt the government into moving
against him.

For a while he was disappointed, for the government paid no
attention to him. But on June 16, 1918, in Canton, Ohio, Debs gave
an address to the Ohio convention of the Socialist party that ultimately landed him in federal prison. There was little in the speech
that he had not said many times in other speeches; he mentioned
war only once; but since he said enough to satisfy the government
that it had a case against him, he was indicted for violating the
Sedition Act on ten counts. His arrest at the end of June sent a
violent shock wave throughout the country.

Debs and his lawyers did not work very hard to secure an acquit-
tal. Their position was simply that the Canton speech was not criminal and that the Sedition Act was in violation of the First Amend-
ment. Debs was not willing to take back anything that he had said or
to deny anything that the government had attempted to prove, and
the defense called no witnesses. The Socialist leader was allowed to
make his own plea to the jury, and he took advantage of the opportunity to speak for almost two hours. He admitted all that had been
testified to in the trial and yet did not feel guilty. "From the beginning of the war to this day," he declared, "I have never by word or
act been guilty of the charges embraced in this indictment. If I have
criticized, if I have condemned, it is because I believe it to be my
duty, and that it was my right to do so under the laws of the land. I
have had ample precedents for my attitude. This country has been
engaged in a number of wars and every one of them has been
condemned by some of the people, among them some of the most
eminent men of their time. . . ." The constitutional right of free
speech was the right he exercised at Canton; "and for the exercise of

that right, I now have to answer to this indictment. I believe in the right of free speech, in war as well as in peace. I would not under any circumstances gag the lips of my bitterest enemy. I would under no circumstances suppress free speech. It is far more dangerous to attempt to gag the people than to allow them to speak freely what is in their hearts."[8]

It came as no surprise to Debs that he was found guilty of trying to obstruct the draft law. In a final, moving statement to the court, he reaffirmed his opposition to capitalism and his devotion to Socialism. "I am opposing," he said, "a social order in which it is possible for one man who does absolutely nothing that is useful, to amass a fortune of hundreds of millions of dollars, while millions of men and women who work all the days of their lives secure barely enough for a wretched existence." But the Socialist movement was strong; and he was optimistic about the future, certain "that the time is coming, in spite of all opposition, all persecution, when this emancipating gospel will spread among all the peoples, and when this minority will become the triumphant majority and, sweeping into power, inaugurate the greatest social and economic change in history."[9] At the conclusion of this statement, he was sentenced to ten years in prison.

An appeal to reverse the decision was rejected by the United States Supreme Court in March, 1919; and Debs was imprisoned the following month at Moundsville, West Virginia. A few months later he was transferred to the federal prison at Atlanta, Georgia. Although this imprisonment was not so idyllic as his sojourn had been at Woodstock, Illinois, in 1895, Debs was no ordinary convict; and he was treated accordingly in both prisons. At Moundsville, he was assigned officially to light duty in the prison hospital; but he in fact did as he wished, and his cell door was never locked. Regulations governing the number of visitors, the writing of letters, and the receiving of radical publications were relaxed for him. When he was transferred to Atlanta, he refused another hospital job and worked instead in the prison-clothing warehouse. Although his correspondence was restricted, regulations concerning visitors and mail were relaxed as they had been in the West Virginia prison. These special privileges were not resented by the other inmates, and his virtually irresistible personality made him a great favorite among the convicts.

Debs's confinement at Atlanta did not prevent the Socialist party from nominating him in 1920 to be its presidential candidate for the fifth time. It was the first time that an American presidential campaign had been conducted from a prison. Although he did not fully approve of the Socialist platform, Debs accepted the nomination, no doubt feeling that he might unite a badly divided party. In 1919, the left wing of the Socialist party had abandoned its old comrades to form two rival groups: the Communist party and Communist Labor party. The result was an American radical movement in shambles. Debs was not ready to join the Communists, although they did their best to woo him; but, at the same time, he disapproved of Socialist criticism of the Communists. Many of his friends had joined the new parties, and Debs was reluctant to oppose them in spite of their desertion of the Socialist party.

Although hopes were high in some Socialist circles for a large vote in 1920, many had their doubts. And the results were not encouraging. Debs received 919,000 votes, only slightly more than had been cast for him in 1912, although women voted for the first time in 1920. The percentage figure was much lower: 3.5 percent as opposed to almost 6 percent in 1912. Yet it was no small measure of Debs's appeal that nearly a million people wanted this imprisoned radical to be their President.

Even before Debs was imprisoned, a campaign had begun to secure his release and that of all other political prisoners. But, while Woodrow Wilson remained President, the Socialist leader never had a chance. A recommendation by the attorney general for a commutation of Debs's sentence was denied by the President shortly before he left the White House in 1921. "While the flower of American youth was pouring out its blood to vindicate the cause of civilization," Wilson declared, "this man, Debs, stood behind the lines, sniping, attacking, and denouncing them. . . . This man was a traitor to his country and he will never be pardoned during my administration."[10]

When Warren G. Harding became President, the attitude changed considerably; and, although some Harding advisors were still opposed to releasing Debs, the new President was determined to do it. In December, 1921, when Debs and twenty-three other political prisoners were set free, the esteem in which Debs was held by his fellow prisoners was made movingly evident as he left the prison. The scene is best described by Debs himself:

Midway in the reservation, between the prison entrance and the street, we were halted by what seemed a rumbling of the earth as if shaken by some violent explosion. It was a roar of voices—the hoarse voices of a caged human host that had forgotten how to cheer and gave vent to their long pent-up emotions in thunder volleys I never heard before and never shall again, for that overwhelming, bewildering scene, without a parallel in prison history, will never be re-enacted in my life. . . . My own heart almost ceased to beat. I felt myself overwhelmed with painful and saddening emotions. The impulse again seized me to turn back. I had no right to leave. Those tearful, haunting faces, pressing against the barred prison windows—how they appealed to me—and accused me!

But I had to go. As I stepped into the waiting car and waved my last farewell another mighty shout was heard. And then another and another and still another, until far, far up the winding road and far away from the terrible prison, the last faint echo of the convict-host that wept as it cheered, died away in the distance.[11]

After a visit to the White House at Harding's request, Debs returned to Terre Haute to a scene not unlike his previous release from jail twenty-five years before as twenty-five thousand well-wishers shouted a "welcome home."

III *The Final Years*

The five years of life that were left to Debs after his release from prison were not ones of great achievements. Obviously, his best years were now behind him. His health had deteriorated during the prison experience, and for the remainder of his life taking care of his health was one of his major concerns. But he was not completely inactive during this period. Poor health had never stopped Debs for long and it did not now. He was continually besieged by visitors; he produced a series of articles about his prison experience with the help of another writer; he was a contributing editor of *Liberator,* a left-wing magazine; and he edited for a brief time a new weekly newspaper, the *American Appeal.* He even broke his long abstinence from holding office in the Socialist party and in 1923 became its national chairman. Fundamentally a speaker, the lure of the lecture circuit again beckoned as he sought to build up the rapidly deteriorating party, but his trip was not quite the same as in the old days. On a tour in 1923 he was frequently greeted with hostility, and he encountered a problem that was new to him: he was unable to secure the prominent auditoriums for his speeches, although he always found somewhere to speak and large crowds came to listen.

For Debs, who had given so much of himself to the cause of Socialism, who had so many grand hopes and expectations for the success of the movement, it must have been painful to witness the collapse of the Socialist party in the 1920's. But he never gave up. In the year before his death, when he was approaching seventy years of age, he lectured in various parts of the country trying to rebuild the local party branches. And much of his oratorical power remained.

Always the champion of the underdog, especially the radical who was suffering unjustly at the hands of the corrupt capitalist judicial system, one of the last of Debs's causes was the Sacco-Vanzetti case. Convicted of murder in Massachusetts in 1921, Nicola Sacco and Bartolomeo Vanzetti were, it was believed by many, really suffering because of their anarchistic beliefs. By 1926, they had managed to avoid execution because of their many defenders, one of whom was Debs. Thwarted by his lecture managers from visiting Vanzetti in prison and thus publicizing the campaign for a new trial, Debs, nevertheless, wrote powerfully in defense of the two anarchists. "It does not matter what the occupation of the worker may be, what he is in theory or belief, what union or party he belongs to," Debs declared in the *Labor Defender* for July, 1926, "this is the supreme cause of us all and the call comes to each one of us and to all of us to unite from coast to coast in every state and throughout the whole country to protest in thunder tones against the consummation of that foul and damning crime against labor in the once proud state of Massachusetts." He called for "a thousand protest meetings" and for "a million letters of indignant resentment" to be sent to the governor of Massachusetts and to Congress. "It is this, and this alone, that will save Sacco and Vanzetti."[12] No doubt he was thinking of another, more successful campaign twenty years before and of Haywood, Moyer, and Pettibone when he wrote. But this campaign was to fail since neither Debs's efforts nor those of other multitudes of defenders could prevent the execution of Sacco and Vanzetti in 1927.

Debs was to have no other causes. In March, 1926, he was forced to give up his work on the *American Appeal* and take his ailing wife to Bermuda. Worry about illness in his family compounded his own frail condition, and a heart attack in the fall led to his death on October 20, 1926. The great expression of grief and the multitude of eulogies that followed Debs's death were not confined to radicals. Men of wealth rubbed elbows with workingmen at his funeral, for he had been a man who could inspire admiration in those who were never convinced by his oratory. "No better epitaph could be found to inscribe over the grave of Eugene V. Debs than 'He Loved His Fellow Man,' " the Chicago *Evening Post* editorialized. "We did not agree with him, but we could not help admiring him. Into our strong disapproval of his views entered a feeling of affection for the man who held them. . . . He thought from the heart, and his heart was always moved by the suffering and misfortunes of the underdog."[13]

According to the New York *Evening World*, "No one could know him and hate him. No one could know him and have contempt for him. It was easy to regret his political course, but no one could doubt the sincerity of his course."[14] And the Los Angeles *Record* described him as "a kindly man so sensitively attuned to the lives of his fellows that their suffering became his own personal pain, driving him into impassioned speech and action on their behalf. . . . No man touched Gene Debs personally who hated him—you just can't hate a human being who takes you unto himself without reservation the way Debs did."[15]

Although the cause to which Debs devoted his life did not culminate in the glorious victory for which he had so arduously striven, a person who was so highly regarded—on whom so many words of praise were lavished—can hardly be considered a personal failure. As one writer declared, "It will be long before another man holds such complete sway over the hearts of common folk."[16]

CHAPTER 4

The Debs Style

BEFORE considering the ideas that Debs put forth in his speeches and writings, it seems appropriate to devote some attention to the combination of characteristics that resulted in a unique individual—in other words, the Debs style. An orator of great power with a deep-rooted sense of history, he made use of every device, including a blatant appeal to the emotions, to win converts to his cause. Although some of his language leaves much to be desired, one cannot doubt his sincerity, his devotion to Socialism, and his unshakable conviction that it would eventually be victorious.

I *The Orator*

Although Debs wrote a great deal, he was first and foremost an orator—an orator of the first rank. In one of his most characteristic poses, Debs is on the edge of a lecture platform, bent at the waist, leaning out into the audience as if he could not get close enough to his listeners, and gesturing vigorously. The sincerity and the intentness of his expression give the impression that convincing his audience of the point that he is making is the most important thing in his life.

He once wrote an article on oratory for *The Coming Nation* in which he explained the "secret" of good speaking. What is most important, he declared, is "having something efficient to express and being so filled with it that it expresses itself. The choice of words is not important since efficient expression, the result of efficient thinking, chooses its own words, moulds and fashions its own sentences, and creates a diction suited to its own purposes." His own abilities in this area, he pointed out, were not due to education or training but to the fact that he had a retentive memory and liked to memorize and deliver speeches and poems that appealed to him.

And reading helped: "I observed the structure and studied the composition of every paragraph and every sentence, and when one appeared striking to me, owing to its perfection of style or phrasing, I read it a second time or perhaps committed it to memory. . . ." But he could not get away from the subject matter of a speech; it was of the greatest importance if one were to express himself effectively. "He who aspires to master the art of expression must first of all consecrate himself completely to some great cause, and the greatest cause of all is the cause of humanity," he wrote. "He must learn to feel deeply and think clearly to express himself eloquently. He must be absolutely true to the best that is in him, if he has to stand alone."

Because Debs was so caught up in his own "great cause," it is not surprising that Socialism crept into the article. It was very difficult for him to write anything without making at least an oblique reference to the Socialist movement: "The most thrilling and inspiring oratory, the most powerful and impressive eloquence is the voice of the disinherited, the oppressed, the suffering and submerged; it is the voice of poverty and misery, of rags and crusts, of wretchedness and despair; the voice of humanity crying to the infinite; the voice that resounds throughout the earth and reaches heaven; the voice that awakens the conscience of the race and proclaims the truths that fill the world with light and liberty and love."[1] There is no doubt that Debs practiced what he preached. He was "filled" with his subject, firmly convinced that he was right, and determined to convince others. His was a powerful combination.

To fellow radical Elizabeth Gurley Flynn, listening to Debs speak was an experience one could not forget. "He was a matchless orator," she wrote. "No one who heard Debs came away entirely unaffected. People who came merely from curiosity were held spellbound by his torrent of burning eloquence."[2] Flynn's sentiments were echoed by another radical colleague, Robert Hunter, who was particularly impressed by a speech that Debs made in Chicago to an audience made up mainly of foreigners who understood little English. "As I heard his beautiful words and saw their wistful earnest faces," Hunter wrote, "I felt that something more powerful, penetrating, and articulate than mere words was passing between the audience and the speaker." To Hunter, Debs seemed able to communicate with his audience in spite of the language barrier. "I remember how my heart beat and how tears began to flow from my boyish eyes. I was ashamed for fear someone would see me. And it was not because of anything that 'Gene was saying. It was solely because of something back of the man, something greater than the man, something bigger, more powerful, and moving than any words or expression." After the speech was over, Hunter approached Debs and "fondled him as I would my own brother." As they left together, the Biblical words of Ruth kept running through his head: "Intreat me not to leave thee, or to return from following after thee: for whither thou goest, I will go, and whither thou lodgest, I will lodge."[3]

II *Debs's Use of Language*

While no question exists about Debs's effectiveness on the lecture platform, his prose is less impressive to read. It is easy to agree with Heywood Broun's statement that Deb's speeches came through as "second-rate utterances" to the reader. An important ingredient was missing when Debs himself was missing, Broun pointed out; and "those speeches of his which seemed to any reader indifferent stuff, took on vitality from his presence."[4]

Debs was capable of using vivid, effective imagery, but he too often descended to depths of excessively flowery language and sloppy sentimentalism. These qualities are found so frequently in his writing that one is hard-pressed to select the most representative, but perhaps one of the best examples of Debs's prose at its purplest is a passage from an article on the "Outlook for Socialism in the United States" written for the *International Socialist Review* in 1900. When he referred to the wars that were ravaging the Philippines and South Africa at the turn of the century, he indicated that, in spite of such "sanguinary scenes," hope for the world existed because "the light of Socialism" is on the horizon. "The skies of the East are even now aglow with the dawn; its coming is heralded by the dispelling of shadows, of darkness and gloom. From the first tremulous scintillation that gilds the horizon to the sublime march to meridian splendor the light increases till in mighty flood it pours upon the world."[5]

Debs's problem was that he didn't know when to stop. He became a prisoner of his descriptive phrases, unable to dam the outpouring of words that continued to flow from his pen long after the job had been done. Nowhere in his writings is this made clearer than in a speech given in Chicago following his release from the Woodstock jail in 1895. Debs informed his audience that his days in jail had been busy ones and that the time for thinking was at night, or rather, as he put it, "when the daily task was over and Night's sable curtains enveloped the world in darkness, relieved only by the sentinel stars and the earth's silver satellite 'walking in lovely beauty to her midnight throne.' "[6] Perhaps this statement was effective when Debs delivered it, but it does not impress the reader.

Debs's flowery language was often accompanied by shameless sentimentalism. In an article entitled "How I Became a Socialist," which appeared in the *New York Comrade* in 1902, he wrote that during his early years he

was nourished at Fountain Proletaire. I drank deeply of its waters and every particle of my tissue became saturated with the spirit of the working class. I had fired an engine and been stung by the exposure and hardship of the rail. I was with the boys in their weary watches, at the broken engine's side and often helped to bear their bruised and bleeding bodies back to wife and child again. How could I but feel the burden of their wrongs? How could the seed of agitation fail to take deep root in my heart?[7]

At no time was Debs more sentimental than when he was concerned with women and children. "Childhood! What a holy theme!" he wrote in 1905. "Flowers they are, with souls in them, and if on this earth man has a sacred charge, a holy obligation, it is to these tender buds and blossoms of humanity." He likened the young victims of poverty and the vicious child-labor system to flowers which are "prematurely plucked" and "fade and die and are trampled in the mire. Many millions of them have been snatched from the cradle and stolen from their play to be fed to the forces that turn a workingman's blood into a capitalist's gold, and many millions of others have been crushed and perverted into filth for the slums and food for the potter's field."[8] At another time Debs declared in a speech that

we have millions of children, who, in their early, tender years, are seized in the iron clutch of capitalism, when they ought to be upon the playground, or at school; when they ought to be in the sunlight, when they ought to have wholesome food and enjoy the fresh atmosphere they are forced into the industrial dungeons and there they are riveted to the machines; they feed the insatiate monsters and become as living cogs in the revolving wheels. They are literally fed to industry to produce profits. They are dwarfed and deformed, mentally, morally and physically; they have no chance in life. . . .[9]

Debs could also be carried away on the subject of women. When he devoted an entire article to women in 1920, he wrote that "In a world that God made beautiful there is nothing so beautiful as woman; and without her divine ministrations, all things would speedily lose their charm. It is woman who bears the future in her body, and on her sweet and sacred bosom nurses life into higher forms and nobler ways. There is nothing so wonderful as motherhood. There is nothing more sacred, more divine than womanhood charged with the future destiny of the race, which means the weal or woe of all that breathe."[10]

With this lofty view of women, it is not surprising that Debs lamented their suffering, just as he grieved for the children who were victims of capitalist exploitation. In a 1905 speech, Debs pointed out the steps by which working class girls often descended into prostitution. "This may be your child," he said. "And if you are a workingman, and this should fall to the lot of the innocent blue-eyed child that you love more than you do your own life—I want you to realize that if such a horror be written in the book of fate, that you are responsible for it, if you use or misuse your power to perpetuate the capitalist system and working class slavery."[11]

It should be said in defense of Debs that he was using sentimentalism as a tool to reach the group he felt must be convinced if Socialism was to have a chance to prevail in the United States. It is frequently difficult for the most rational of people to resist the old tug at the heartstrings if it is skillfully applied—and Debs was a master. Many a worker must have been profoundly moved by imagining his daughter as the girl driven to prostitution by the capitalist system. Certainly it is safe to say that the language Debs used in the cause of Socialism did not stop the people from coming to hear his speeches.

III   Debs's Sense of History

Throughout his life Debs was moved by a strong sense of history, and his writings and speeches are liberally sprinkled with references to the past, especially to the radical past. Inasmuch as he styled himself a revolutionary, it is not surprising that he looked to bygone revolutionists and revolutionary movements in search of analogies to his own time. "Let us glorify today the revolutions of the past," he wrote in 1907, and he then quoted what he referred to as Mark Twain's "royal tribute to the French Revolution": "the ever memorable and blessed revolution, which swept a thousand years of

villainy away in one swift tidal wave of blood—one: a settlement of
that hoary debt in the proportion of half a drop of blood for each
hogshead of it that had been pressed by slow tortures out of that
people in the weary stretch of ten centuries of wrong and shame and
misery the like of which was not to be mated but in hell."[12]

But Debs most frequently made reference to the American
past, especially to the American Revolution. Nearly ten years before
his conversion to Socialism, he wrote in the *Locomotive Firemen's
Magazine* that "The Nation had for its cornerstone a strike."[13] He
meant, of course, the Revolution. The traditional American heroes
of the Revolution were among his favorite people in history, and he
mentioned them frequently in his writings and speeches. For
example, in one of the articles by Debs about the Haywood, Moyer,
Pettibone affair that appeared in the *Appeal to Reason*, he wrote:
"In the course of history and the sweep of events great crises develop on the eve of great social changes, and in every such crisis
great characters, born of the revolution and expressing its spirit,
appear upon the stage of action, take the heroic parts assigned to
them and write their names in imperishable deeds in the history of
humanity."

Haywood, Moyer, and Pettibone fell into this category, he believed, like Patrick Henry, Samuel Adams, and John Hancock before the war for American Independence. "These men were all
loathed, hated, denounced and persecuted in the name of 'law and
order' and 'the peace of society,' of which they were supposed to be
the relentless enemies. . . . Patrick Henry was denounced by King
George and William Haywood by President Theodore [Roosevelt].
Both Henry and Haywood incarnated the subject class, espoused its
cause, voiced its protest and defied the ruling class, and this has
always been denounced as 'treason' and never more fiercely than
today."[14]

On a number of other occasions, Debs made reference to the
American Revolution. He found a parallel to the American experience in the struggle of Mexicans to free themselves from the
tyranny of Porfirio Diaz, for Debs believed that the Mexican revolutionists "were animated by the same passion for freedom as
were the American revolutionists a century and a half ago and with
far greater justification for resisting tyranny and oppression." Certain Mexican revolutionaries who were imprisoned in the United
States, he declared, were "traitors to Mexico, even as Franklin,

Paine, Jefferson and Patrick Henry were traitors to Great Britain."[15] A few months later Debs again wrote of the imprisoned Mexicans, and two Russian rebels who were also jailed in America. "What would James Otis and Patrick Henry say to these liberty-loving and self-sacrificing spirits in American jails, guarded by Mexican and Russian bloodhounds?" he asked. "Their eyes would again flash fire as they launched the thunderbolts of their wrath upon the despotism of the tyrant and the degeneracy of the people. But these are the days of Rockefeller, not Jefferson; Morgan, not Paine; Carnegie, not Kosciusko."[16]

During Debs's famous 1918 trial, he again invoked the spirit of the American Revolution and found similarities between the 1770's and his own day—between the patriots of the Revolution and the Socialists of the early twentieth century. "When great changes occur in history, when great principles are involved, as a rule the majority are wrong," he declared in his address to the jury. "The minority are usually right. In every age there have been a few heroic souls who have been in advance of their time, who have been misunderstood, maligned, persecuted, sometimes put to death. Long after their martyrdom monuments were erected to them and garlands woven from their graves. . . ." At the time of the American Revolution, he continued, the great majority of the American colonists remained loyal to the king and to the divine right theory of government.

But there were a few men in that day who said "We don't need a king; we can govern ourselves." And they began an agitation that has immortalized them in history. Washington, Jefferson, Franklin, Paine and their compeers were the rebels of their day. When they began to chafe under the rule of a foreign king and to sow the seed of resistance among the colonists they were opposed by the people and denounced by the press. . . . But they had the moral courage to be true to their convictions, to stand erect and defy all the forces of reaction and detraction; and that is why their names shine in history, and why the great respectable majority of their day sleep in forgotten graves. . . .[17]

Along with the Revolution, the other great radical experience in the American past was the Abolition movement, and Debs was fond of comparing those who sought to end the system of chattel slavery before the Civil War with those later Abolitionists whose target was wage slavery. This attitude was also a line he pursued prior to his adoption of Socialism. In an 1887 *Locomotive Firemen's Magazine* editorial entitled "Abolitionists," he pointed out that those who wanted to abolish injustice did not disappear with the freeing of the slaves. Debs felt that a revolution was in progress, but he did not yet regard it as a revolution to change the form of government but as one "to make government, courts and institutions subserve the happiness of the American people." Indeed, his Abolitionists were those who "point to the wrongs and say they must disappear. . . ."[18]

In the *Appeal to Reason* article quoted above, in which Debs likened Haywood, Moyer, and Pettibone to the heroes of the American Revolution, he also made reference to the Abolitionists. "But Haywood is charged with murder," he wrote. "So was John Brown; and he never denied it. John Brown was the sworn enemy of the slave holders. He spat upon their 'morals' and held their laws in contempt. He not only advocated violence and incited bloodshed, but led in both, and yet many of the best men and women living today regard this 'monster of depravity' as the grandest man, the loftiest soul, the sublimest hero that ever walked the earth."[19]

In addition to Brown, whom Debs often mentioned in glowing terms, he had great admiration for another Abolitionist, Wendell Phillips. At the time of the Fred Warren prosecution, the Socialist leader pointed out that the *Appeal* editor "has the same contempt for the supreme court of today that Wendell Phillips had for the supreme court half a century ago."[20] On another occasion, during the same struggle between Warren and the courts, Debs likened the attack on the *Appeal to Reason* to the early nineteenth-century attacks on William Lloyd Garrison's Abolitionist newspaper *The Liberator*, to which Phillips was a frequent contributor. He stressed that "Wendell Phillips, the dauntless champion whose centenary has just been celebrated, and whose place is secure among the immortals, had often to fight not only to prevent free speech from being strangled, but for his very life. Were Phillips among us today he would be at the very head and front of the fight the *Appeal to Reason* is making to prevent a capitalist government from sandbagging it into silence."[21]

In another article, in which Debs urged the members of the United Mine Workers and of the Western Federation of Miners to arm themselves against "Rockefeller's private army of assassins," Debs again referred to the famous Abolitionist. "Wendell Phillips declared that it was the glory of honest man to trample bad laws under foot with contempt," he stated, "and it is equally their glory to protect themselves in their lawful rights when those who rule the law fail to give them such protection."[22] In Debs's address to the jury in 1918, he declared that "William Lloyd Garrison, Wendell Phillips, Elizabeth Cady Stanton, Susan B. Anthony, Gerrit Smith, Thaddeus Stevens and other leaders of the Abolition movement who were regarded as public enemies and treated accordingly, were true to their faith and stood their ground. They are all in history. You are now teaching your children to revere their memories, while all of their detractors are in oblivion."[23]

For the most part, Debs used history to illustrate the present by seeking parallels in America's radical past, but he strayed on at least one occasion from his main point to philosophize in a rather superficial way about the writing of history. Even here, his purpose was to draw an analogy, for he was comparing the case of Fred Warren with that of John Peter Zenger, the eighteenth-century newspaper publisher whose historic trial for libel in 1735 was a landmark in the history of freedom of the press in the United States. Both Warren and Zenger, Debs pointed out, attacked the ruling power; both were arrested. Reading about the Zenger case led Debs to reflect on the writing of history in general. "Written history," he declared, "is unceasingly at work revising itself. It requires hundreds, sometimes thousands of years for the truths of history to be correctly chronicled. As with events so with the characters who participate in them." Events and leaders that seem of great importance today, he continued, "shrivel away as they recede in the distance, whereas other events, deemed of slight consequence, and other men who attracted little attention, or were perhaps regarded as evil-doers, loom larger and ever larger in the perspective until finally, when all the facts are clearly understood and all the truths are correctly written, history appears almost as a tissue of self-contradictions."[24].

Debs displayed no profound knowledge of history, but he was very much aware of America's past and made use of it in his campaign to educate the people in the benefits of Socialism. He saw himself and his fellow Socialists as carrying on a long tradition of radicalism in America that stretched back to the Revolution. Just as the patriots of the 1770's struggled to liberate the colonists from the tyranny of Great Britain and just as the Abolitionists of the pre-Civil War period fought to liberate the Blacks from the slave aristocracy of the South, the Socialists were striving to free the modern victims of injustice—the workers—from the clutches of capitalism.

IV *The Optimist*

Examples of Debs's optimism are so abundant in his writings and speeches that the reader often encounters it in portions of his speeches that have been quoted in this study but that have dealt primarily with other topics. But optimism is so fundamental to his thinking, so significant a facet of his outlook on life, that no chapter that purports to deal with the Debs's style can omit consideration of it.

Traces of this optimism appear early in his writings, although they are frequently tempered with a somewhat pessimistic view of man. In 1884, while editor of the *Locomotive Firemen's Magazine*, Debs wrote that "we are by no means doubtful of the future, indeed, we are confident that the best will survive." But the main theme of this editorial was that "self-interest is the controlling force in human affairs. Only those who indulge in utopian dreams anticipate at an early day universal agreement in matters pertaining to the general concerns of life." Such agreement is not only unattainable, it is undesirable, he wrote. "It would be productive of monotony and stagnation. . . . We do not, therefore, anticipate the immediate development of any new phases of human nature. . . ."[25]

This reference was not the only one that Debs made to the inflexibility of human nature. "If there are those who believe that human nature has undergone any radical change since our first parents ate the forbidden fruit," he wrote a few years later, "they are, to put it mildly, the victims of an hallucination too serious in influences for jest or raillery." Human nature had its good and bad elements, but normally the bad side makes its appearance. "From savagery up through all the gradations to the highest civilization, we find human nature exhibiting its native characteristics, greed, war, conquest and oppression; the strong lording it over the weak, crushing and degrading them, compelling them in numberless ways to pay tribute. . . ." And yet it cannot be said that the tone of this article is entirely defeatist and pessimistic, for he was arguing for federation of the railway brotherhoods which he hoped would help the railroad worker to improve his lot. And his statement that the good elements in human nature could be brought forth with "indomitable patience, inspired by hopes that will not down at the bidding of adversity. . . ." suggests a latent optimism.[26]

In 1895, Debs dealt with the matter of optimism more directly and excluded himself from the category. "The optimistic school of philosophers who believe, or affect to believe, that all things are ordered for the best, look abroad and say the present conditions are 'well enough and ought to be let alone' ", he wrote. "Their faith is stupefying. . . . In all the ages of the world the optimist has in human affairs symbolized inertness. . . . If the colonists had been optimists, Massachusetts would still be hanging witches and whipping Quakers and Americans would be subjects of Victoria."27 But even here, when he seemed to be so obviously rejecting optimism, Debs is not really the pessimist he appears to be. For he was arguing for government ownership of railroads and telegraph facilities which would, he believed, make life easier for millions of people. The problem lies in the definition of optimism. In this instance, Debs was using the word to describe those who were satisfied with the *status quo* in America—those who liked what they saw about them and resisted change. But a better definition, and one that more nearly describes optimism in the American experience, is a belief that, however bad things are, they are bound to get better—that all problems will be solved and that some day the Kingdom of God will be achieved on earth. This kind of optimist Debs became, and one can find strains of this brand of optimism in his pre-Socialist writings even if one frequently must look beneath a pessimistic overlay to find it.

Sometimes it is not necessary to look beneath the surface, as is the case with Debs's "Proclamation to the American Railway Union" which was written at about the same time as his attack on "optimists." June, 1895, was not a time for Debs to be optimistic. The Pullman Strike had recently been smashed, his beloved American Railway Union was all but destroyed, and he had been sentenced to six months in jail. And yet he could hold out hope to the remnants of his battered union: "Our faith in the future of our great order is as strong as when our banners waved triumphantly over the Great Northern from St. Paul to the coast. Our order is still the undaunted friend of the toiling masses and our battle-cry now, as ever is the emancipation of labor from degrading, starving, and enslaving conditions. We have not lost faith in the ultimate triumph of truth over perjury, of justice over wrong, however exalted may be the stations of those who perpetrate the outrages."28

Inasmuch as it is difficult to imagine one who seeks fundamental change having no hope for the future, it is not surprising that Debs revealed a sparkling optimism after his conversion to Socialism. In the writing and speaking that he did for the rest of his life, he almost always displayed his deep-seated conviction that the adoption of the Socialist system would bring forth significant improvements in the human condition. Very early in his career as a Socialist, Debs declared that, under the new economic system for which he intended to work, "there would be work and plenty for all, reasonable hours and life would be something more and better than a prolonged agony or a continuous curse. Another panic would never curse the land. Crime would disappear and suicide would cease to shock the public conscience."[29] On another occasion he pointed out that present conditions were not natural and, inasmuch as they were created by men, could be changed by men. Just as humanity can be degraded, he wrote, it can also be elevated.[30] In 1905, he declared that, if the workers would join the newly formed Industrial Workers of the World, they would become "the rulers of this earth. They will build houses and live in them; they will plant vineyards and enjoy the fruits thereof. The labor question will have been settled, and the working class, emancipated from the fetters of wage-slavery, will begin the real work of civilizing the human race."[31]

There was almost no end to the evils Socialism would eradicate and to the advantages it would bestow on civilization. At one time or another during Debs's career, he predicted that "the army of tramps will be disbanded" and that "prisons will be depopulated."[32] He foresaw an end to "the prostitution of womanhood, and the murder of childhood," and he believed that "women shall be the comrades and equals of men, sharing with them on equal terms the opportunities as well as the responsibilities, the benefits as well as the burdens of civilized life."[33] Socialism would also mean the "end of war" and the "inauguration of the reign of peace on earth and good will toward all men."[34]

Debs, who once wrote disparagingly of utopian dreamers and who had doubted that human nature could change, evolved into an unabashed optimist and something of a utopian himself. Perhaps this facet of his outlook is best described in a statement that he wrote for the *Appeal to Reason* in 1907: "Looking backward over the last thirty years, the progress of the labor movement can be clearly traced, and its contemplation is fruitful of inexpressible satisfaction. Looking forward, the skies are bright and all the tongues of the future proclaim the glad tidings of the coming Emancipation."[35]

In the Debs style, his sense of history, his optimism, and his oratorical gifts—laced frequently with an obtrusive but not ineffective sentimentalism—were an integral part of Debs's efforts to spread his ideas throughout the country.

CHAPTER 5

Socialism and the Labor Movement

THE last twenty-five years of Eugene Debs's life were devoted to the development and dissemination of his ideas about Socialism and the labor movement. During these years of struggle, Debs became firmly convinced that a combination of political and economic action was necessary to rescue civilization from the hands of the capitalist exploiters. If the Socialists were to be successful, not only would they have to continue to seek control of government through party victories, but they would also have to be active in the labor movement, especially in the development of industrial unions. Only such a two-pronged attack on the citadel of capitalism would result in the millennium.

I Socialist Ideas

In the years that followed Debs's conversion to Socialism, he adopted a Socialist philosophy that remained virtually unchanged to the end of his life. Although he refined it and made slight alterations in detail, he continued to espouse the same brand of Socialism throughout his career. Unlike some radicals—such as onetime Socialist leader Algie M. Simons who ended his working years writing for the American Medical Association—Debs did not seem to grow more conservative as he grew older.

Basic to his thinking was the Marxian concept of the class struggle—the division of society into two antagonistic groups. Debs had not always felt this way, for many of his pieces that appeared in the *Locomotive Firemen's Magazine* during his editorship argue against the idea of class struggle. Debs's early opposition to strikes was coupled to a belief that "the interests of employer and employed are identical. . . . The employer puts in the capital, the employee furnishes the labor. . . . Any harm done to capital injures labor, and any harm done to labor injures capital."

He believed at the time that an important objective of the Brotherhood of Locomotive Firemen was to prevent unnecessary conflict between employer and employed. "One of our fundamental doctrines," he wrote, "is that labor and capital are brothers. With hand in hand they march along the highway of progress, and it is wrong and suicidal to put them at enmity." Those who have attempted to open a breach between capital and labor have done so for selfish reasons and should be ignored. "Some have gone so far as to say that there is a natural, a necessary conflict between labor and capital," he went on. "These are very shallow thinkers, or else very great demagogues."[1] Characteristically, Debs looked to the future with a full measure of optimism. "We are to hear less in future about the war between labor and capital," he wrote, "because such a war is the creation of diseased brains. Such a war does not exist, and in the nature of things can not and never did have an existence."[2]

Debs seemed to see a distinction between capital and labor, on the one hand, and those individuals representing capital and labor on the other. "The conflict is not between capital and labor, between money and misery, cash and credit," he insisted in 1887, "it is between man and man, the man who works and the man who pays, the man who employs and the man employed."[3] A few years later he declared that "Capital is the creation of labor, and to talk of war between capital and labor, finds its parallel in the assumption that the hand wars against the eyes, or vice versa. The trouble in the past has been between *capitalists* and *workingmen;* the former seeking to crush the latter. . . ."

But Debs was quick to assert that not all capitalists were to be condemned: "There are many men controlling capital, who recognize in workingmen, their best friends. They pay liberally and promptly, and as a general proposition, they are successful in their business."[4] These were the words of a man who was still working within the existing system. It was not capitalism that was at fault, but some of the men who operated the capitalist system. "The revolution now in progress," he wrote in 1887, "is not to change the form of government . . . but rather to make government, courts and institutions subserve the happiness of the American people."[5]

An important element of Debs's conversion was his abandonment of trying to work within the system, for he began to believe that little was more important for Socialist victory than for the workers to grasp the idea that they must unite as one group to oppose and defeat the capitalists. "The one thing above all others for the workingman to see and understand is the class struggle," he wrote in 1903. "The very instant he grasps this fact his feet are on the rock—he takes his place with his class and, come what will, he holds it, especially on election day. . . ."[6] Two years later he again declared: "The most important fact in all the world for workingmen to take cognizance of is the class struggle. . . . The working class are in an overwhelming majority. They have the numbers. They ought to have the power. And they would have the power if only they were conscious of their interests *as a class*."[7] Perhaps because he realized the difficulty involved in making American workers class-conscious—and the failure to do so seems to be one of the important factors in the fruitless efforts of the Socialists to achieve victory in the United States—Debs constantly hammered this point home in his speeches and writings.

In view of the fact that Debs believed one of the most important tasks of those seeking the triumph of Socialism was to convince the workers of their class interests, it is not surprising that he should feel that education was an important function of the Socialist party. His interest in making certain that Socialists were well informed was made clear in his plans for a good newspaper and for a publishing house for the Social Democracy of America in 1897. His views did not change in the following years. "Ignorance alone stands in the way of Socialist success," he declared during the presidential campaign of 1904.[8] In the process of education, the press, he felt, was especially important; in fact, he regarded the labor press as "paramount to all other agencies and influences. . . ."[9] "The primal need of the working class is education," he stated again in a 1905 speech. "By education I mean revolutionary education; the kind that enables men to see that the twenty-odd millions of wage workers in the United States are wage-slaves. . . ."[10] Debs obviously had something in mind besides an academic education, but educating the workers to unite as a class and to oppose capitalism was fundamental to a Socialist victory, and thus he looked upon it as his primary mission.

In countless speeches and writings, Debs defined the system that properly informed, class-conscious workers could put into effect. Socialism, he explained in 1900, "means the collective ownership by all the people of all the means of wealth production and distribution. . . . Socialism does not propose the collective ownership of property, but of capital; that is to say, the instruments of wealth production, which, in the form of private property, enable a few capitalists to exploit vast numbers of workers, thus creating millionaires and mendicants and inaugurating class rule and all its odious and undemocratic distinctions." He maintained that, because Socialism would allow no one to have private property upon which others depended for employment, "industrial mastery and slavery would disappear together and competition for profit would give way to co-operation for use."[11] But Debs denied that the Socialists intended to destroy private property completely. "We are going to establish private property," he declared in 1908, "all the private property necessary to house man, keep him in comfort and satisfy his wants. Eighty percent of the people of the United States have no property today. A few have got it all. They have dispossessed the people, and when we get into power we will dispossess them."[12]

Early in Debs's career as a Socialist, he identified himself with the left wing of the movement by making clear that he wanted nothing to do with reform groups. "The battle royal is now on," he wrote in 1898. "It is between Capitalism and Socialism; there is no middle ground and there can be no compromise."[13] Two years later he declared "The Social Democratic party is not a reform party, but a revolutionary party. It does not propose to modify the competitive system but abolish it. . . ."[14] When, in 1903, Henry Demarest Lloyd wrote to Debs to ask him if he felt Socialists could cooperate with reformers in a local Chicago dispute, the Socialist leader was definite in his reply: "No, I do not believe that single taxers, socialists and anti-socialist trade unionists can successfully harmonize upon any proposition whatsoever. In some exigency they may do so for the moment, but when it comes to formulating plans and platforms and shaping policies they are bound to separate for they are fundamentally antagonistic and every attempt to unite them, even temporarily, has resulted in failure and generally bitter feeling besides."[15]

Debs's continued concern about keeping the Socialist party a truly revolutionary one is evidenced by an article entitled "Danger Ahead" which appeared in the *International Socialist Review* in 1911. In it, he indicated that the large increase in the Socialist vote in the elections of 1910 was not entirely pleasing to him because he believed that some of the votes "were obtained by methods not consistent with the principles of a revolutionary party, and in the long run will do more harm than good." He feared that the Socialist party would become "permeated and corrupted with the spirit of bourgeois reform to an extent that will practically destroy its virility and efficiency as a revolutionary organization." He had no desire to attract votes to the party if this meant modifying revolutionary principles. "These votes do not express Socialism," he wrote, "and in the next ensuing election are quite as apt to be turned against us, and it is better that they be not cast for the Socialist Party, registering a degree of progress the party is not entitled to and indicating a political position the party is unable to sustain."[16]

II *Debs and Violence*

A basic question that anyone committed to the overthrow of an existing system must ultimately encounter concerns the methods he intends to use. The extent to which Debs was committed to violence is not easily determined, for his statements on the subject are anything but consistent. One who wishes to show that Debs favored achieving the cooperative commonwealth by violent means can do so by selecting carefully from the Socialist leader's writings and speeches. On the other hand, the writer who seeks to present Debs as a man of peace can also do so by making a different selection. The truth, therefore, is elusive. But a close study of the sources leaves the impression that fundamentally Debs abhorred violence; was driven to advocating violence only on isolated, extreme occasions; and sincerely wished to reach his Socialist goal peacefully through the democratic process.

There is no denying the fact that on a number of occasions in his career as a Socialist, Debs called for, or at least threatened, violent measures. "There has got to be a social revolution," he wrote in 1899, "a complete wiping out of capitalism, peaceable *or otherwise* [italics added], and any compromise at this stage is fatal."[17] Three years later, during the coal strike of 1902, he conjured up the specter of violence when he declared that, "if ever the barricades are thrown up in the streets of New York and Pennsylvania by an insurgent mob and that bunch of coal barons find themselves tied back to back in the death cart on the way to the guillotine, they may seek comfort in the reflection that they are reaping the harvest sown by their own bloody hands."[18] And, in a 1905 speech supporting industrial unionism, Debs exhorted the workers to "strike together, vote together and, if necessary, fight together."[19]

But Debs could become more vehement than such a statement indicates. Perhaps his best-known violent statements are in "Arouse, Ye Slaves" which appeared in the *Appeal to Reason* on March 10, 1906. Occupying the middle three columns from top to bottom of the newspaper's front page, the words leaped at the reader as if written in fire. "The latest and boldest stroke of the plutocracy," he began, "but for the blindness of the people, would have startled the nation." He was referring to the arrest and extradition from Colorado to Idaho of Bill Haywood, Charles Moyer, and George Pettibone for the murder of former Governor Frank Steunenberg of Idaho.

Debs was obviously incensed. Haywood and Moyer were officials of the radical Western Federation of Miners, and the Socialist leader regarded their treatment as a threat to the whole labor movement. "It is a foul plot," he wrote, "a damnable conspiracy; a hellish outrage." He insisted that the accused men were innocent of the charge against them and that their arrest was merely an attempt to remove their obnoxious presence by those they had opposed. Debs saw a parallel with the Haymarket affair that had occurred twenty years earlier when "the capitalist tyrants put some innocent men to death for standing up to labor." But times had changed since that tragedy; and, "if an attempt is made to repeat it, there will be a revolution and I will do all in my power to precipitate it."

This case was an issue upon which the whole labor movement could and must unite, Debs maintained, "for we cannot desert our comrades and allow them to be put to death. If they can be murdered without cause so can we, and so will we be dealt with at the pleasure of these tyrants." There were no alternatives left, Debs believed, but forcible resistance since the courts could not be depended upon to do anything for the workers. Specifically, he proposed a revolutionary convention and, if necessary, "a general strike could be ordered and industry paralyzed as a preliminary to a general uprising. . . . They have driven us to the wall and now let us rally our forces and face them and fight," he wrote. "If they attempt to murder Moyer, Haywood and their brothers, a million revolutionists, at least, will meet them with guns."[20]

There is little question about the fact that Debs seemed ready to fight in March, 1906, and additional evidence of a tendency toward violence can be found. On many occasions Debs defended men associated with violence, both in the past and in his own day. One of his greatest heroes was the Abolitionist John Brown. The fact that Brown had participated in the bloody Pottawatomi massacre in Kansas before his abortive plan to free the slaves through violent means did not prevent Debs from depicting him as "the bravest man and most self-sacrificing soul in American history. . . ." who "set an example of moral courage and of singlehearted devotion to an ideal for all men and for all ages."[21] And at another time he wrote: "John Brown was the sworn enemy of the slave holders. He spat upon their 'morals' and held their laws in contempt. He not only advocated violence and incited bloodshed, but led in both, and yet many of the best men and women living today regard this 'monster of depravity' as the grandest man, the loftiest soul, the sublimest hero that ever walked the earth."[22]

Debs was also vigorous in his defense of the McNamara brothers—the two men, officials of the Structural Iron Workers, who were charged with blowing up the *Los Angeles Times* building during a strike in October, 1910. The explosion destroyed the building and caused the deaths of twenty persons as well as injuries to another seventeen. Debs, convinced that the McNamaras had been framed, defended them vigorously both in the columns of the *Appeal* and on the lecture platform. But the campaign to free the two brothers suffered a severe blow when the McNamaras confessed their guilt. Although their confession was undoubtedly a blow to Debs, he defiantly wrote that "We Socialists are making no apology for any word or deed of ours in the McNamara case, and as for myself personally I shall not denounce them. I condemn the crime, but I pity all the victims, all of them, the McNamaras included. . . . I have not changed my mind about the theory that the dynamiting of the *Los Angeles Times* was instigated by the capitalists themselves. I am convinced that all these dynamiting crimes had their inspiration in capitalist sources and their genesis in capitalist camps."[23]

Clashes between striking miners and company guards in various parts of the country early in the twentieth century brought forth Debs's ire and caused him to advocate meeting violence with violence. In one such confrontation in 1914, Arkansas miners on strike engaged in a gun battle with guards and defeated them. In addition, considerable damage was done to the mines with dynamite; and Debs was jubilant. "Bravo, ye coal-digging slaves of the pits!" he wrote. "You have done your duty in a heroic manner and deserve the applause of all honest men." Debs called for other

miners to follow their example and suggested that the United Mine
Workers and the Western Federation of Miners establish a defense
fund so that every member of the unions could be supplied with a
rifle and ammunition. Gatling and machine guns should also be
purchased by the unions to enable the miners to defend themselves,
he believed.[24]

There is still more evidence of Debs's tendency toward violence
that is perhaps less dramatic but nevertheless significant. In an
article entitled "Sound Socialist Tactics," which appeared in the
International Socialist Review for February, 1912, Debs informed
his readers that he had no respect for capitalist property laws and
that, if he had the force to overthrow these laws, he "would use it
without an instant's hesitation or delay. . . ." The workers, he
believed, had a right to use any weapon that would help them win
their fight against capitalism.[25] In September, 1915, he stated that
he was against every war but one: "the world-wide war of the social
revolution. In that war I am prepared to fight in any way the ruling
class may make necessary, even to the barricades."[26] And, later in
the year, he called on the workers to "declare war" on the capitalists
when the latter declare war on one another, to "paralyze industry by
the general strike, and [to] fight every battle for the overthrow of
the ruling class. . . ."[27]

The case for Debs as an advocate of violent means to secure the
triumph of the workers and the destruction of the capitalist system
is, as far as it goes, a substantial one. But at least as good a case can
be made for Debs as a vigorous opponent of violence; and this
position can be supported, at least in part, by selections from some
of the same writings and speeches that have already been quoted.
Although Debs referred countless times, to Socialism as a
revolutionary movement, it by no means follows that he had in mind
violent revolution. In fact, it would appear that in the great majority
of instances when he used the word, he thought of it as meaning
simply drastic change. He seemed to regard the word "revolution"
as the opposite of "reform," and he used it to make clear that he
would not settle for a mere change in the capitalistic system; he
demanded a complete overthrow of it—an overthrow that was to be
effected peacefully by using the democratic process. As Debs asserted in a 1904 speech, the historic mission of the Socialist party
was "to conquer capitalism on the political battle-field. . . ."[28]
Perhaps the best evidence of all to demonstrate what Debs meant

when he referred to Socialism as a revolutionary movement is suggested by his mention of Jesus as the "revolutionary Savior"[29] he was. It is hardly likely that he thought of Jesus as a violent man.

On more than one occasion Debs preferred to use the word "evolution," and this word more accurately describes the method by which his "revolution" was to be effected. "Capitalism has had its day . . . ," he wrote in 1900, "and must now give way, by the inexorable law of economic revolution, to its successor. . . ," Socialism.[30] Debs expanded on this idea in a 1909 article in which he explained the Marxian concept of the inevitability of Socialist revolution. "The coming of Socialism is not a matter of speculative philosophy, but of scientific demonstration," he declared. "It is a philosophy of history, based upon the laws underlying social development. Karl Marx, the founder of Socialism, did not invent Socialism, but merely discovered the laws of social progress which must inevitably bring Socialism." Socialist Debs explained that capitalism was but one temporary phase in the history of civilization, that it had "entered upon its declining stages," and that it was on the way out while Socialism was coming to replace it. "In a word," he concluded, "it is a matter of development. The forces underlying society are never at rest. The same forces which produced capitalism are now operating to displace it and to produce as its successor a more perfect social order."[31]

Debs insisted, time and time again, that he was not in favor of violence; and what is probably his most complete discussion of this subject appeared in the 1912 article "Sound Socialist Tactics." After stating, as mentioned above, that he would break the law if he had the power and that the workers had a right to use any weapon against capitalism, he devoted most of the article to an argument *against* the use of violence. He opposed the use of force, he said, because violence was not a weapon that would help the workers to win. Not only did it have a demoralizing effect upon the followers of those who practiced it, but it was also likely to boomerang and hurt, not help, their cause. "If sabotage and direct action, as I interpret them, were incorporated in the tactics of the Socialist Party," he declared, "it would at once be the signal for all the *agents provocateurs* and police spies in the country to join the party and get busy." The Socialist party would be held responsible for the actions of every spy or madman; and the result would be a disrupted, disunited party, that would be "the despair of the betrayed workers

and the delight of their triumphant masters." He admitted, however, that some emergency situations might justify violence, but its
use certainly should not be general party policy.[32]

Debs accompanied some of his most vehement calls for violence
on the part of the workers with statements of his fundamental belief
in peace. In "Arouse, Ye Slaves", he insisted that the workers were
not responsible for the situation. "It has been forced upon us," he
wrote, "and for the very reason that we deprecate violence and
abhor bloodshed we cannot desert our comrades and allow them to
be put to death."[33] A later article that also dealt with the Moyer,
Haywood, and Pettibone affair contained a denial that the supporters of the three accused men favored violence. "We are not opposed
to law and order," Debs insisted. "We are opposed to the shams and
hypocrisies; the frauds and crimes that resist threatened exposure as
an attack upon 'law and order.' "[34] And, in the case of the Arkansas
miners, Debs asserted that he and the Socialists were opposed to
violence "except when lawless violence is forced upon us and we are
compelled to fight for our lives in defense of our homes and
families."[35]

In his later years, Debs continued to make statements opposing
violence. Although his reaction to the Russian Revolution is considered later in more detail, it should be mentioned here that Debs
was not favorably inclined toward the blood-letting that accompanied it.[36] After his release from prison in the early 1920's, he told
his writer-friend David Karsner that "Violence begets violence and
a social system such as ours, that is maintained by force and violence, may be destroyed by force and violence. I hope the change
may be accomplished by peaceful means. I have always urged it that
way. I believe in political action as a means of meeting the present
demands for social change." When pressed by Karsner, Debs admitted that, if the Socialists won an election and if the capitalists
refused to turn over the government, "the capitalist system would
have to be wiped out on the battlefields." But he would not like to
be in a position where he would have to order anyone to war.[37] And
it is difficult to characterize as aught but a man of peace one who
states quite baldly that he can find "no extenuating circumstances
that would allow me to take the life of my bitterest enemy. . . ."[38]

After such an array of opposing viewpoints, it seems obvious that,
on the subject of violence, Debs was pulled in two different
directions—a not unusual human condition. Fundamentally, he was

a man of peace who firmly believed that the Socialist triumph, in America anyway, could be effected by the ballot box. And yet there were clearly many times in his career when he seemed to feel that violence, or at least the threat of violence, was necessary—that peaceful means simply would not serve the purposes of the workers. Certainly, when war is made on striking miners, they must defend themselves. When union officials are being railroaded to the executioner, the workers must come quickly to their defense. How serious he was about calling for armed revolt in connection with the Haywood, Moyer, Pettibone affair remains a question, especially in view of a letter he wrote to the *Appeal to Reason* the year after "Arouse, Ye Slaves" had appeared. Debs stated in his letter that, "If we cannot arouse the people sufficiently to threaten revolt on a large scale[,] they are gone."[39] Was not what he really wanted merely the threat of revolt? One other piece of evidence supports this interpretation. During an interview with Debs in 1908, Lincoln Steffens asked the Socialist leader why he had called for a mob to rescue Moyer, Haywood, and Pettibone two years before? " 'Why, my God, man, that was only a cry,' " Debs replied. " 'That was pain. . . . I sometimes think I am destined to do some wild and foolish, useless thing like that and—so go.' "[40]

In addition to these special situations, there seem to have been other occasions throughout his life when Debs had some doubts about the efficacy of peaceful methods—when he was ready to "go to the barricades" if there was no other way to achieve what he was determined to achieve. But, although he was not being entirely candid when he told David Karsner that he had "always" urged peaceful change and when he stated flatly in his address to the jury in the Canton trial that "I have never advocated violence in any form,"[41] there is little doubt that Debs, in his more sober, reflective moments, looked toward a Socialist victory without resort to violence.

III *Debs and the Labor Movement*

Debs began his career as a labor leader; and, while his conversion to Socialism caused him to concentrate his activities on political action, he always remained interested in union affairs. Never did he cease to believe that the defeat of capitalism would be effected through both economic and political organization. One of the fundamental causes of division in the Socialist movement during the

early years of the twentieth century was the controversy that raged
over the relationship between Socialism and the labor movement.
There were two basic schools of thought. One held that the interests
of the Socialist party would best be served by securing control of
existing unions and the American Federation of Labor; this attitude
was called "boring from within." Others, including Debs, who were
opposed to the AFL's exclusion of all but skilled workers, considered "boring from within" to be hopeless; their plan was to abandon
the Federation and to support a militant labor movement based on
industrial unionism.

Those who favored industrial unionism at the turn of the century
tended to look to the miners of the West for support. The Western
Federation of Miners, which had been founded in 1893, had been
involved in a series of violent strikes throughout the decade, including those at Cripple Creek and Leadville in Colorado and at
Coeur D'Alene in Idaho. During its first ten years, the Federation
won a number of strikes and boosted its membership to fifty
thousand. In a desire to expand, it affiliated with the American
Federation of Labor in 1896; but it withdrew the following year. In
1898, still seeking allies, the Western Federation of Miners formed
the Western Labor Union which, four years later, became the
American Labor Union, and it attempted, rather fruitlessly as it
turned out, to establish itself as a rival to the American Federation
of Labor.

Because of the focus of these Western unions on industrial
unionism and because the American Labor Union adopted the
Socialist party platform, Debs was a hearty supporter of this Western labor movement and had harsh words for Socialists who would
not support it. "This radical departure from the effete and reactionary non-political policy of the American Federation of Labor, so
long and so earnestly striven for by the Western leaders, and so
entirely compatible with the Socialist conception of class-
consciousness and progressive trades-unionism, should have been
met with the prompt and hearty approbation of every unionist and
every Socialist in the land," he wrote in November, 1902. But such
approval had not been granted. The party had turned its back upon
the "young, virile, class-conscious union movement of the West"
and was "fawning at the feet of the 'pure and simple' movement of
the East. . . ."

Debs was vehement in his condemnation of the American

Federation of Labor. This organization should support Socialism, he maintained, and ought to eliminate its leaders "who secure fat offices for themselves in reward for keeping the rank and file in political ignorance and industrial slavery. . . ." Moreover, the organization should "cease to rely upon cringing lobbying committees, begging, like Lazarus at the gate of Dives, for a bone from a capitalist legislature and Congress it helped to elect. . . ." But, in spite of Debs's biting denunciation of the AFL, Debs insisted, at this time, that he did not wish to destroy the organization; he simply wanted to "bring it up to date and have it, as it must become if it is to survive, a class-conscious industrial union, its members recognizing the Socialist ballot as the weapon of their class and using it accordingly, thus escaping the incongruities and self-contradictions of the present 'pure and simple' union, whose members strike against the boycott and the effects of the capitalist system while voting industriously to perpetuate the system."[42]

Debs's position regarding organized labor and the role of labor in the overthrow of the capitalist regime remained substantially the same throughout the remainder of his career. The two themes—support of industrial unionism and opposition to Samuel Gompers and the American Federation of Labor—appear in many of his writings and speeches. Such views were expounded in an important article entitled "Unionism and Socialism" which appeared in the *Appeal to Reason* in 1904 and which was published as a pamphlet later in the year. In it, he made clear his belief that the craft union was outmoded in the advanced industrial age of the twentieth century. "A modern industrial plant has a hundred trades and parts of trades represented in its working force," he wrote. "To have these workers parcelled out to a hundred unions is to divide and not to organize them, to give them over to factions and petty leadership and leave them an easy prey to the machinations of the enemy." Instead, all workers in a given plant ought to belong to one union— "This is the industrial plan, the modern method applied to modern conditions, and it will in time prevail."[43]

In view of Debs's devotion to the cause of industrial unionism, it is not surprising to find him among the founders of the Industrial Workers of the World. This most radical of American labor organizations had its inception at a conference called late in 1904 by leaders of the Western Federation of Miners. Twenty-three persons from a variety of unions and radical organizations attended, including Debs. The conference issued a statement of principles which denounced the American Federation of Labor and called for the establishment of one great industrial union. All interested labor groups were invited to a convention to meet in June, 1905; and this convention, attended by about two hundred delegates, founded the Industrial Workers of the World. All workers would belong to the same union, in contrast to the federation concept of the AFL, but the new labor organization would be divided into thirteen departments covering all industries in the country.

In a speech before the Industrial Workers of the World (IWW) convention, Debs lashed the American trade union movement in general and the AFL in particular. The movement, he felt, was controlled by the capitalists and was being used for their purposes. No longer did he have hopes that the AFL might be converted to an industrial union. "There are those who believe that this form of unionism can be changed from within," he declared. "They are very greatly mistaken. We might as well have remained in the Republican and Democratic parties and have expected to effect certain changes from within. . . ." Debs believed that to be successful the new labor organization must be based upon the class struggle and be "totally uncompromising." It was important that the Industrial Workers of the World be "so organized and so guided as to appeal to the intelligence of the workers of the country everywhere." If such an organization is formed, he maintained, "its success is a foregone conclusion." He looked forward to a time, "and not a long time at that," when there would be "a single union upon the economic field," as well as "a single party upon the political field; the one the economic expression, the other the political expression of the working class; the two halves that represent the organic whole of the labor movement."[44]

That Debs's attitude toward the AFL was not mere rhetoric is supported by a private letter that he wrote shortly after the IWW had been established. "I have not one bit of use for the AF of L," he declared. "It belongs to the capitalists and they are running it and will continue to run it. . . ." Although some 'Socialists still believed they could make an industrial union out of it, he stated, "I not only look upon this as impossible but absurd."[45] Very clearly, Debs had lost confidence in the AFL by 1905. Those Socialists who continued to place their hopes on "boring from within" the AFL were opposed to the IWW, despite its radical nature, because they saw it as causing a serious division in the labor movement. Debs had no patience with such allegations. "Of all the silly and stupid charges," he wrote, "the one that we are 'splitting' the trade union movement takes the palm."[46]

Late in 1905, Debs made a series of speeches in New York and Chicago in which he elaborated on his position regarding craft versus industrial unionism, vigorously supported the IWW, and urged his listeners to join it. He reiterated his belief that the craft union was no longer adequate to meet the demands of the workers. This type of union, he declared, "is now positively reactionary, and is maintained, not in the interests of the workers who support it, but in the interests of the capitalist class who exploit the workers who support it."[47] Workers must, above all, recognize the existence of the class struggle—they must realize that the capitalist and the worker have nothing in common and that the capitalist must be overthrown for workers to achieve a complete victory. "We have organized the Industrial Workers for the purpose of uniting the working class; the whole working class," he maintained. "Not only the skilled workers, not only those who are favored, but the working class, skilled and unskilled, male and female, in every department of activity, are united upon the principle of Industrial Unionism."[48]

After all workers were united in the one organization, Debs explained, the central and most important function of the IWW was to prepare them to take over and operate the industries.[49] The new organization would do all that it could for the worker under the capitalist system, "but while it is engaged in doing that, its revolutionary eye will be fixed upon the goal; and there will be a great difference between a strike of revolutionary workers and a strike of ignorant trade unionists who but vaguely understand what they want and do not know how to get that."[50]

Debs's enthusiasm for the IWW, so exuberant in the 1905 speeches, waned over the years; and he ultimately disassociated himself from that organization. He seems to have been suggesting one reason for his desertion of the IWW when he wrote in 1910 that he was opposed to trying to destroy the old unions even though they were obsolete, reactionary, and hostile to Socialism. He believed that trying to destroy them would only strengthen them and their leaders. "It should be distinctly understood," he declared, "that to smash the existing unions and establish industrial unions by force. . . ." ought not to be the mission of an industrial union.

Although he did not refer to the IWW by name at this time, there is little doubt that he had it in mind.[51] Probably an important reason for his increasingly frigid attitude toward the IWW was its tendency to abandon politics. If the organization "had continued as it began," he wrote in 1914, "a revolutionary industrial union, recognizing the need of political as well as industrial action, instead of being hamstrung by its own leaders and converted, officially at least, into an anti-political machine, it would today be the most formidable labor organization in America, if not the world." Those who opposed political action were anarchists, Debs believed, and there was little hope for anarchists and Socialists to work together.[52]

In spite of Debs's disaffection for the Industrial Workers of the World, his constant interest in the unity of the radical movement led him to continue to support the organization against outside attacks. These attacks were especially severe after the entry of the United States into World War I; and in February, 1918, Debs published the article "The I.W.W. Bogey" in the *International Socialist Review*. He wrote: "I think I may claim to be fairly well informed as to the methods and tactics of the I.W.W.—with some of which I am not at all in agreement—and I have no hesitancy in branding the sweeping criminal charges made against them since the war was declared as utterly false and malicious and without so much as a shadow of foundation in fact." Referring to the assertion that the IWW was planning to sabotage factories and crops, he asked: "Was a more stupendous lie or a more stupid one ever hatched in a human brain?"[53] Again, in the Canton, Ohio, speech of June, 1918, he declared that he had "great respect for the I.W.W."[54]

This defense of the IWW in its time of troubles did not mean that Debs had reconciled his differences about the tactics of that organization. But he had not changed his mind about the virtues of industrial unionism either. "Industrial unionism is the only effective means of economic organization," he wrote in 1910; "and the quicker the workers realize this and unite within one compact body for the good of all, the sooner will they cease to be the victims of ward-heeling labor politicians and accomplish something of actual benefit to themselves and those dependent upon them."[55] By 1914 Debs seemed somewhat discouraged about the slow advance of industrial unionism. "There must needs be further industrial evolution," he declared, "and still greater economic pressure brought to bear upon the workers in the struggle with their masters, to force them to disregard the dividing lines of their craft unions and make common cause with their fellow-workers."[56] But Debs remained, as usual, optimistic about the future; and he did not cease his efforts to bring about effective industrial unionism. In his Canton speech of 1918 he again exhorted the workers to "Organize industrially and make your organization complete."[57] And, after his release from prison in the early 1920's, he was speaking in a similar manner. The steel, mine, and railroad strikes of the postwar period had ended in defeat, he wrote in 1923, because the workers "fought under a craft union instead of an industrial union standard. . . ." Craft unionism was "a crime against the working class. Its sole purpose in the present industrial development is to keep the workers divided, arrayed against each other for the benefit of their masters and misleaders, and to their own detriment and undoing. . . ." The craft union was obsolete, originally designed to protect the worker in small shops; and, as industry grew, the craft union should have been converted into an industrial union. But he was not advocating dual unionism, he insisted, for "the lessons of past experience warn against any such further attempt. The rank and file must insist upon getting together and must furnish the impetus for such concentration and combination as are necessary to unite all the workers of a given industry within one compact and militant body."[58]

There was no change in Debs's attitude toward the American Federation of Labor as a result of his disappointment with the IWW. In 1911, he warned against cooperation with "reactionary trade-unionists in local emergencies and in certain temporary situations to effect some specific purpose, which may or may not be in harmony with our revolutionary program." He would accept the support of trade unionists who believed in Socialism, but this certainly did not include the AFL which was "deadly hostile to the Socialist Party. . . . To kow-tow to this organization and to join hands with its leaders to secure political favors can only result in compromising our principles and bringing disaster to the party."[59] One reason for the weakness of Socialism in Chicago, he believed, was the fact that the movement "has catered too much, in her eagerness to catch votes and subscribers, to the reactionary trade unions and the corrupt influences which dominate these aggregations of disunion and reaction."[60]

Debs's attack on craft unionism and on the American Federation of Labor frequently took the form of personal attacks on the AFL president, Samuel Gompers. Debs's attacks may have originated in Gomper's refusal to support the Pullman Strike in 1894, but the union leader's dislike of Socialism would undoubtedly have been sufficient to arouse Debs's ire. Whatever the reason, Gompers suffered at the pen of Debs. In 1911, Gompers came off second best when Debs compared him with *Appeal to Reason* editor Fred Warren. Both men were on trial; but, while Warren, to Debs's delight, denounced the court as the enemy of the working class, "Gompers has been mumbling his apologetic excuses like an old woman in the hands of a constable, fearing to utter a word of protest, or sound a note of challenge, lest he give offense to the corporation attorneys who have been put upon what is called the 'bench' to declare the crimes of capitalists lawful and the lawful acts of workingmen crimes."

The Socialist leader's description of the contrast between the attitudes of the two men was striking. Warren's stance before the court was "erect, defiant, inspiring," Debs wrote; but "Gompers crawls at its feet and whines like a spaniel. Warren is the real champion of the working class, the true leader of the people; Gompers sits on the shirt-tail of the labor movement yelling 'whoa,' afraid to keep up with it and afraid it will get away from him."[61] In 1919, Debs characterized the deportation of aliens following mass arrests of radicals carried out under the direction of Attorney General A. Mitchell Palmer as an "atrocious exhibition of capitalist despotism" which he blamed on "Chief Gompers and his scabbing and strikebreaking craft unions, which are simply auxiliary to the Wall Street power."[62] Thus it would seem that Gompers took more than his share of the blame from Debs for the opposition encountered by the radical movement in the United States.

Debs's views on Socialism and the labor movement were central to his thought during his entire career, but they did not occupy all of his attention. Although he never lost sight of the ultimate goal—the victory of Socialism—Debs frequently expressed ideas about other matters of significance to him; and the coming of World War I was especially important in bringing to the fore some new problems for him to deal with.

CHAPTER 6

Debs and World War I: Pacifism and Communism

WORLD War I affected Eugene V. Debs in two important ways. First, it elicited from him a powerful statement of his basic opposition to war. Although this position had been formed long before, it was more strongly stated during the 1914–18 conflict, and it rivaled in its frequency the usual Socialist propaganda that people had come to expect in his writing and speeches. Second, World War I helped make possible the Russian Revolution, which had important repercussions for the American Socialists. The victory of Communism in Russia contributed to a fatal split in the Socialist movement in the United States, and this situation confronted Debs with a difficult decision.

I The Pacifist

Because of Debs's many demands that the people violently redress their grievances against the capitalists, it is, perhaps, not entirely accurate to consider him a pacifist. Yet his opposition to most wars is undeniable. Inasmuch as he felt that they were the products of capitalism in which the lower classes suffered and died primarily for the benefit of their capitalist masters, he saw no reason to support them. War and its concomitants, militarism and imperialism, did not occupy so much of his attention as other topics basic to the Socialist program; but his references to them are scattered throughout his writings from his years as a labor editor to the end of his life. As is to be expected, anti-war statements bulk particularly large during World War I; and his opposition to American involvement in that conflict represents one of the most significant events of his life.

Before Debs's conversion to Socialism, his hostility toward war had not yet hardened; for in the *Locomotive Firemen's Magazine* for August, 1885, he wrote that American wars "have been for the right, forced by circumstances. . . ." But, even at this early date, his editorial argued vehemently against a standing army, the purpose of which, he felt, was to "shoot down strikers. . . ." And his bitterness about militarism was apparent in his attitude toward the United States Military Academy:

It has long been known that the influence of West Point upon society has been vicious in the extreme. As a general proposition, the graduates of that institution are insufferable snobs. They have the idea drilled into them that they constitute a ruling class. They are supported off of the earnings of the people, and acquire a strut and swagger indicative of feelings of superiority, at once disgusting and humiliating, and the knowledge that they are life pensioners upon the government adds indefinitely to their offensive superciliousness. West Point annually inflicts upon the country a great horde of these gold-lace parasites, public crib loungers, who toil not, and for whose services there is neither a present or a remote necessity.

Debs was disturbed because there were people in the United States who wanted, in addition to the "useless burden" of West Pointers, "a military establishment larger than that which obeys the nod of any European despot. . . ." to be ready for labor troubles. "Laboring men, everywhere throughout the broad land, may well regard the movement with deep concern. It means their ultimate subjugation. It is to bring on a conflict between bread and bullets, pay and powder."[1] A year later he wrote again on the same subject. "Standing armies always and everywhere are the foes of liberty," he declared. "They are terrible machines operated by despots to crush out the aspirations of the masses for liberty. . . ."[2]

In 1898, following the termination of hostilities between the United States and Spain, Debs called for a speedy reduction of the military to peacetime size. The country had been able to progress satisfactorily for a century with only the nucleus of a regular army; therefore, he implied, it would be able to continue without one in the future. Furthermore, a large standing army was not only unnecessary, but dangerous. "In a historical sense the main point of difference between a despotism and a democracy is the standing army," he wrote. "Where there is a despotism there is a standing army, and where there is a standing army there is a despotism." He was optimistic enough to believe that "slowly but steadily we are emerging from the savagery of war," a happy event that would be consummated with the victory of Socialism over capitalism. But such a victory had not yet occurred, and Debs did not really expect the reduction of the army to be carried out quickly. "The commercial spirit, born of the capitalist system," he declared, "requires a large standing army to maintain its regime and enforce its edicts, and as congress is subservient to its will the army will remain a fixed and permanent, if not the central and controlling, factor in our government. . . ."[3]

Debs adopted an anti-imperialist stance in his attitude toward the territories taken from Spain during the war. He advocated the establishment of a temporary protectorate over Cuba, Puerto Rico, and the Philippines until a government was established. Then the people of these islands should be allowed to decide for themselves whether they wanted independence or annexation to the United States.[4] His anti-imperialism was modified, however, in regard to Hawaii which, although not taken from Spain, was annexed at the time of the Spanish-American War. Debs did not object to the annexation of Hawaii because the inhabitants were in part white and had already established a government.[5]

Between 1898 and the outbreak of World War I, occasional anti-war statements can be found in Debs's writing and speeches. In a 1909 article entitled "War is Murder in Uniform," he characterized war as an "adjunct to wholesale and persistent robbery committed under the organization falsely called civilization." The motive for all wars, except for revolutions, had always been robbery, he declared. At one time the man of wealth was the victim; but, "since capitalism has come to dominance, the victim is not the merchant, unless he be a foreigner, but the farmer and factory worker, who produced the wealth that was taken." Debs concluded with an urgent plea for the common people to stop participating in capitalistic wars, "for if the workers shall cease to kill each other for others' gain, the monstrosity of war will pass away like a horror of the troubled night."[6] On another occasion, the Socialist leader denounced a proposal to institute military training in high schools as "adding murder to the curriculum of our public school system." He also advocated the circulation of anti-war pledges which would bind the signer to refuse "to shoulder a gun or any other deadly weapon for the purpose of killing his fellow man under any circumstances whatsoever. . . ."[7]

With the beginning of World War I in 1914, Debs became in-

creasingly concerned about war and militarism. Long before the
United States became a participant, he vehemently proclaimed his
opposition to the conflict and to the preparedness campaign of the
American government. His abhorrence of large standing armies and
of the militarism they tended to foster had not changed from the
time of the Spanish-American War. Preparedness, he declared, was
"nothing less than a monstrous conspiracy, a colossal crime of the
ruling nabobs and their gilded gangsters against the common
people, and once they have the great standing army and the powerful navy they are plotting for, the once vaunted American republic
will be transmogrified into a military oligarchy and the working class
may then bid farewell to the few surviving liberties which have not
been strangled by the courts or crushed by the militia of the
capitalist class."[8]

Debs insisted he was not opposed to all war, but he was opposed
to "ruling class war, for the ruling class is the only class that makes
war. It matters not to me whether this war be offensive or defensive,
or what other lying excuse may be invented for it, I am opposed to
it, and I would be shot for treason before I would enter such a war."[9]
Military training of schoolboys as part of the preparedness movement also drew fire from Debs who saw it as a first step toward
militarism. Such training was undesirable, he felt, because it "develops the military instinct and kindles to flame the base passion for
military glory."[10]

Debs was not disturbed that his opposition to preparedness might
appear to be unpatriotic. When Daniel Hoan, the Socialist mayor of
Milwaukee, defended his participation in what was characterized as
a preparedness parade by claiming that every Socialist was
patriotic—devoting his life to making the country a better place in
which to live—he earned a sharp rebuke from Debs. "I cannot at all
agree to the views regarding patriotism expressed in your communication," he wrote privately to Hoan. "Socialists are not required to
demonstrate their patriotism for the benefit of the capitalist class
and that class will not only not thank them for it but hold them in
greater contempt."[11] And, on another occasion, Debs proclaimed
his allegiance to humanity rather than country when he wrote: "I
have no country to fight for; my country is the earth; I am a citizen of
the world."[12]

In Debs's vitriolic article " 'Preparedness' and Poverty" that appeared in the *American Socialist* in December, 1915, he called upon

the ruling class to "fight their own wars and defend their own booty." The workers owed them nothing and had nothing to protect. "Plutocracy, patriotism, preparedness, poverty and pauperism are interlinked in the military program of Wall Street," he declared; "and if the workers are not totally blind they will steer clear of that devil's snare and launch a scheme of preparedness of their own for the day coming when they will have to fight for their lives, if they are not to be completely crushed beneath the iron hoof of a military autocracy."[13] He had no fear of an attack from without, he wrote to Upton Sinclair a month later. "The invasion and attack I want the workers to prepare to resist and put an end to comes from within, from our own predatory plutocracy right here at home. I don't know of any foreign buccaneers that could come nearer skinning the American workers to the bone than is now being done by the Rockefellers and their pirate pals."[14]

The Socialist leader believed that the United States ought to work hard to bring about an end to the war. This country could, he declared near the end of 1915, "strike a death blow to war . . . by issuing a proclamation of peace—itself setting the example of disarmament to the nations of the world. . . ."[15] But a few months later, while still advocating peace efforts by the United States, he was not optimistic about the likelihood of disarmament. Experience had shown, he maintained, "that capitalist nations have no honor and that the most solemn treaty is but a 'scrap of paper' in their mad rivalry for conquest and plunder"; therefore, even if a disarmament program were adopted, it "might prove abortive and barren of results." As he had in regard to the territories taken from Spain, Debs advocated that the people of the lands conquered in the war should decide by popular vote whether they wanted to be independent or be annexed to another country. But for permanent peace, he insisted, "international industrial democracy" must supplant "national industrial despotism." He never seemed to get away from the fervant belief that the solution to all problems, not excluding war, was the victory of Socialism.[16]

Debs supported the notion of a war referendum given considerable popularity at the time by Allan L. Benson, a prominent Socialist propagandist who replaced Debs as the Socialist candidate for President in 1916. Benson's scheme called for taking the power to declare war away from Congress and giving it to the people. On a day designated by Congress, all men and women over eighteen

would have the right to cast a ballot. The ballots would be signed
and a record kept of the order in which they were cast. If the vote
were in favor of war, those who supported it would be taken into the
army first. If more were needed, those not voting would be enlisted;
and, if this were not enough, more men would be taken from among
those voting against the war, beginning with those who voted latest
in the day.[17] Debs had great respect for the anti-war writings of
Benson in general, and for the war referendum in particular. "The
people of no country have ever yet declared war," Debs wrote, "and
it is a safe assumption that once the people are far enough along to
have the declaration of war in their own hands and to understand
that they who vote for war and declare war must be the first to go to
the front and fight the battles, there will never be another war."[18]

After the United States entered the war in April, 1917, Debs
refused to modify his stand in spite of the fact that many Socialists
chose to support the war and some, including Allan Benson, left the
party in the ensuing split. When the Socialists voted at their
emergency convention in St. Louis shortly after the declaration of
war to oppose the participation of the United States in the conflict,
Debs wholeheartedly supported the position. He denied that such
action was treasonable. "We are neither pro-German nor pro-Ally,"
he wrote in the *American Socialist* shortly after the convention. "We
are Socialists, international Socialists, and we have no use, not one
bit, for capitalist wars. We have no enemies among the workers of
other countries; and no friends among the capitalists of any country. . . . The class war is our war and our only war."[19]

Debs's intransigence landed him in federal prison. Ironically, his
most famous anti-war speech, the Canton, Ohio, address of June,
1918, on which his indictment was based, had very little to say about
American participation in the war. At one point he referred to the
secret treaties revealed by the Bolsheviks after the Russian Revolution, and what he had to say was critical of the European Allies
but hardly of the United States which had not been a party to the
treaties. "I have a copy of these treaties," he declared, "showing
that the purpose of the Allies is exactly the purpose of the Central
Powers, and that is the conquest and spoliation of the weaker nations that has always been the purpose of war." He then condemned
wars in general, but he did not refer to World War I directly. "The
master class has always declared the wars," he wrote; "the subject

class has always fought the battles. The master class has had all to gain and nothing to lose, while the subject class has had nothing to gain and all to lose—especially their lives. . . ." In much the same manner that he had used many times before, Debs pointed out that "the working class who freely shed their blood and furnish the corpses, have never yet had a voice in either declaring war or making peace. It is the ruling class that invariably does both. They alone declare war and they alone make peace."[20]

In the years following World War I, Debs saw the specter of militarism continuing to haunt the country. He was opposed to the Boy and Girl Scout movement because its purpose, he felt, was "to inculcate the military spirit and develop the war psychology in these young boys and girls under the false pretense of solicitude for their health and welfare. . . ."[21] Similarly, he wrote in 1925 that the American Legion sought "to inculcate the military spirit, create a military caste, and promote militarism generally in the United States so that there will be no danger of the Wall Street warlords running short of cannon fodder when they give the signal for the next grand killing."[22] Until his death, Debs remained alert to the dangers of militarism and war which he found inextricably bound up with the capitalist system; and, to him, only Socialism would free the country from the tentacles of these twin monsters.

II *The Dilemma of Communism*

The Russian Revolution of 1917 delighted Debs as it did so many Socialists, for a hated capitalist regime had at last been overthrown and a Socialist government was in power in its place. "The workers of Russia have risen to the demand," he wrote in April, 1918, "and are fighting with a desperation born of the highest resolve to establish the rule of the working class in the former empire of the czar. . . . We shall believe that complete triumph will finally crown the most extraordinary revolution in history and that the light of Russia, so long the land of darkness, will ultimately spread over all the earth."[23] A few months later, in the Canton, Ohio, speech of 1918, Debs again praised "the Bolsheviki of Russia. Those heroic men and women, those unconquerable comrades have by their incomparable valor and sacrifice added fresh lustre to the fame of the international movement."[24] And he wrote early in 1919 in glowing terms of the Russian people and their "fearless, incorruptible and uncompromising" leaders, Vladimir Ilyich Lenin and Leon Trotzky. "From the crown of my head to the soles of my feet I am Bolshevik, and proud of it," he declared.[25]

One of the many results of the Russian Revolution was a split in the American Socialist movement. The stunning victory of a mere eleven thousand Bolsheviks convinced the left wing of the Socialist Party of America that a small group, sufficiently possessed of revolutionary zeal and purity of doctrine, could be successful—that the slow process of winning over a majority of the population, as the right wing sought to do, was not necessary. In 1919, when the growing differences between left- and right-wing members of the American party came to a head, thousands of left wingers were either expelled or suspended, and the American Communist movement was born. Not without problems, however, for in the age-old manner of radicals, the leftists could not agree among themselves. The result was the formation of two new political organizations, the Communist party and the Communist Labor party, which existed until 1921 when they joined to form the Communist Party of America.[26]

This fundamental cleavage in the American Socialist movement caused a dilemma for many radicals who were caught in the middle. Should they remain with their present organizations or join the Communists? Debs was one so affected. On many crucial issues his thinking had been in line with that of the left wing of the party. But to go so far as to abandon the party that he had served so faithfully for so long—this was a matter of no little consequence.

There were at least three factors that influenced Debs's final determination about Communism. One involved the unity of the radical movement. Debs deplored factionalism in the movement and had always tried to stay out of factional fights. Thus the splitting of the Socialist party and the formation of two new radical organizations in 1919 did not please him. "Socialists, communists, anarchists, syndicalists and I.W.W. spend more time and energy fighting each other than they do fighting capitalism," he lamented in 1920.[27] The beginning of the American Communist movement occurred after Debs went to prison in 1919; therefore, he was not directly involved.

Soon after his release in December, 1921, Debs was urged by the Socialist party to make a statement in which he pledged his continued allegiance to that organization. Representatives of the Communist and Workers parties also sought his support. Sick, frustrated by the fragmented movement, he reacted bitterly. "When I entered prison there was a united party," he wrote to Otto Branstetter, national secretary of the Socialist party, in March, 1922. "When I came out it had been torn to pieces. I had nothing to do with it. But promptly on my release I am expected to get into the factional fight, utterly disgusting in some of its phases, and side with everybody against everybody else."[28] Debs agreed to listen to all sides before taking a position, but his precarious health prevented his doing so immediately after his release. It is clear, however, that his dislike of factionalism and his great desire for unity of the radical movement prejudiced him against new parties whose establishment only weakened that movement.

Another factor that was influential in determining Debs's attitude toward Communism was the behavior of Soviet leaders. Although Debs continued to view the Russian Revolution as a whole favorably, he was profoundly disturbed by some aspects of the movement—especially by the violent excesses of the Soviets. He was horrified by the execution of the Czar and his family; he stated, according to the recollection of his writer friend, David Karsner, "My blood boiled when I read the other day of the heinous murder of the czar, his wife and daughters. The crime was of such a revolting nature that it confounds the intelligent sensibilities of anybody who calls himself a Socialist."[29] He was ashamed "that such savagery should be committed in the name of Socialist justice that has for its aim and purpose the setting up of the higher standards of human conduct."[30] And, when it became known that the Bolsheviks were about to execute the members of the Social Revolutionary party, Debs went so far as to send the following cablegram to Lenin: "I protest with all civilized people in the name of our common humanity against the execution of any of the Social Revolutionaries or the unjust denial of their liberty. Soviet Russia can set an example by refusing to follow the practices of worldwide czardom and should uphold the higher standards we seek to erect and profess to observe."[31]

Debs also spoke out against the control that the Soviet leaders were attempting to exert over Socialist parties outside of Russia. When the Third (Communist) International was established in 1919, Debs originally wanted the Socialist party to join it. But the purpose of the Third International was to enforce a uniformity among Com-

munist parties all over the world; and by December, 1920, Debs
had reversed his earlier position. "Since seeing the conditions laid
down by G. Zinoviev, chairman of the Executive Committee of the
Moscow International to the German Independent Socialists and
the Independent Labor Party of Great Britain, I have changed my
mind," he wrote. "No American party of the workers can subscribe
to such conditions and live."[32] After Debs was released from prison,
he elaborated on this position. Each nation is unique, he believed,
with its own problems, and Soviet dictation should not be accepted.
"We can give the Russian Revolution and the Soviet government
every possible support, morally, spiritually and financially," he
stated in June, 1922, "without surrendering our own identity as
American Socialists and workers who have social and industrial
problems peculiar to our national life and with which the average
Russian is wholly unfamiliar."[33] Obviously, Debs was able to per-
ceive, early in the history of the Communist movement, the fundamental weakness that has always afflicted the Communist party in
this country: excessive dependence on the leadership of Moscow.

In addition to the concern Debs felt about the control that the
Soviet leaders were trying to exercise outside of Russia, he also was
beginning to have some doubts about the results of the revolution in
Russia. By 1922, he had come to believe that the Russian people had
merely "swapped dictators," that Lenin, Trotzky, and others were
giving the orders that the Czar once gave. This result was not his
idea of freedom or of Communism. "Russia has no Communism," he
told David Karsner. "Communism presupposes intellectual and
spiritual enlightenment beyond Socialism, and if 80 per cent of
Russians are illiterate can we in truth say and believe that Russia is
intellectually and spiritually advanced over, let us say, England,
America or France?" He regarded Communism as a more advanced
stage of human development than Socialism, but it had to be
reached through Socialism. The process would be slow and
evolutionary, and it was not reasonable to believe "that a country
ridden for centuries by the blackest tyranny can with one gesture
leap into Communism, in which the better, finer and nobler qualities of man would have an opportunity for free and untrammeled
expression."[34]

Finally, Debs's attitude toward Communism was affected by the
nature of the American Communist party. He particularly disliked
the underground character of the party, and he believed that little

could be accomplished by such an approach. To those who reminded him of the underground movement in Russia before the revolution, he answered that Russia was not the United States. If the Socialist party had not been successful after twenty-two years of "overground" work, he pointed out, what chance did the underground efforts of the Communists have? "All my life I have been opposed to secret and whispering organizations," he told Karsner. "There is nothing in them that is beneficial to the workers, and it has been proven time and again that nearly every underground revolutionary movement is honeycombed with spies and agents provocateurs."[35]

By the fall of 1922, Debs was ready to make the eagerly awaited statement about his position regarding Communism and the Communist party. In his statement that appeared in the *New York Call* on October 8, he began by lamenting the division and dissension in the radical movement; and he made it clear that he wanted no part of it. "I have never had any heart for factional warfare," he stated. "I simply cannot and will not engage in it." Debs then explained that, as soon after his release as his health had permitted, he had listened to representatives, had read the literature of each of the various radical factions, and had ultimately concluded that he would remain with his old party. "I see no reason why I should desert the Socialist party now," he declared. "I have spent the better part of my active life in its service and why should I now turn upon it and rend it; seek to tear down, destroy what I have devoted all these years of struggle and persecution helping to build up?"

He admitted that the Socialists had made mistakes, and that he would like to see changes made, but this was true of any party. His decision had been a painful one, he said, for he did not like to see beloved comrades in hostile camps. But he would continue to have respect for the members of the new parties, and he hoped "that in good time the differences that now separate us will be ironed out by the stern logic of events and that we shall be once again united and marching shoulder to shoulder into battle together for the overthrow of capitalism and the emancipation of the workers of the world." In the meantime, he recommended that the Socialist party follow a policy of "harmonious relation" with other radical parties and work with them whenever possible. Above all, the party should concentrate on reconstruction and leave such questions as international affiliation until a later day.

Debs ended his statement with some thoughts about the Russian Revolution. Although he conceded that the Soviets had made some mistakes, his language for the most part was as glowing as it had been when the revolution had first occurred. He stated that the revolution, "in what it expresses for the Russian people and in what it portends for the oppressed and exploited peoples of all nations, is the greatest, most luminous and far reaching achievement in the entire sweep of human history." He had nothing but praise for the Soviet government and its leaders; for Lenin, he believed, was "the greatest thing that came out of the world war. . . ." Debs's conclusion was a trumpet call to international support of the Soviets. "All hail, then, the Russian revolution and the Soviet Government, the crowning glory of the twentieth century!" he wrote. "Let us all unite, East and West, North and South, over all the earth, and pledge our loyal and unqualified support to our Russian Comrades until the irresistible revolution they have inaugurated has run its triumphant course and achieved the peace and freedom of the world!"[36] Although definitely not attracted to the American Communist party in spite of his affection for some of its members and although not entirely satisfied with the course of events in Russia, Debs took great pains to make clear to his radical comrades that his support of the Russian Revolution remained wholehearted.

CHAPTER 7

Debs and the Underdogs

E UGENE Debs became a Socialist primarily because he was a
man of deep compassion who felt that a basic change in the
system was necessary to enable the disadvantaged to climb out of
the depths into which capitalism had driven them. For the most
part, he was concerned about the worker and therefore directed
most of his attention toward the workingman who was not getting
out of the system what he deserved—certainly not what his labor
entitled him to receive. But Debs's sympathy for the underdog, the
dispossessed, those who were trodden upon by society, often turned
him in other directions and led him to champion the causes of other
groups. Among these were convicts, women, and Black Americans.

I Convicts and the Prison System

It is not surprising that a man who was placed behind bars twice
during his lifetime—each time, he felt, unjustly—should be bitter
about prisons. But Debs's views about punishment for convicted
criminals transcended his own experience; for his incarcerations,
both at the Woodstock jail in 1895 and at Moundsville and Atlanta
from 1919 to 1921, were pleasant in comparison with the lot of most
convicts. The Socialist leader became fully convinced of the need for
prison reform, and he wrote extensively on the subject after his
release from Atlanta. This writing took the form of a series of twelve
articles about his prison experience that he prepared for the Bell
Syndicate with the help of a ghost writer, David Karsner. But only
nine were published at the time and these were carefully edited,
for, although Debs had agreed to leave out political opinions, he
found it difficult to do so. All of the articles as Debs had originally
written them, together with some other writings about prisons,
were gathered into a book entitled *Walls and Bars* that was published in 1927, the year after Debs's death.

Debs had not always felt so strongly about the evils of the prison system as he did when he wrote the articles that appeared in *Walls and Bars*. In 1887, when he was editor of the *Locomotive Firemen's Magazine*, an editorial entitled "Prison Labor" had some curious things to say—curious, that is, in view of Debs's later thoughts about criminals and prisons. His concern in 1887 was about the competition that convicts, hired out as laborers, were creating for what he called "honest labor." But, at the same time, he made some statements completely at odds with his later convictions: "The slobbering philanthropy of the times finds expression in ceaseless twaddle about reforming criminals. They would transform prisons into asylums, hospitals, industrial schools, making reformation the primary object of incarceration, and punishment secondary, and this sort of statesmanship and philanthropy, yoked and pulling together, has made many prisons delightful places of resort for a class of criminals who, for moderate terms of confinement, express favorable opinions of the arrangement." Convicts were well treated, he insisted, with "regular and *square* meals, . . . good beds, good clothes, good medicines and doctors, books and papers, moral and religious instruction."[1]

It was not long before Debs's views drastically changed. Although prison reform was not a primary subject of his writings and his speeches prior to the 1922 articles, occasional references to the topic show his point of view. His opinion of capital punishment was made clear in a 1902 article in which he told how, after his arrest during the Pullman Strike of 1894, a jailer at Chicago's Cook County Jail showed him "the blood-stained rope used at the last execution and explained in minutest detail, as he exhibited the gruesome relic, just how the monstrous crime of lawful murder is committed."[2] One of Debs's most quoted statements, which appeared in the *New York Call* in 1914, hinted at his opinion of criminals and imprisonment: "While there is a lower class I am in it; while there is a criminal element I am of it; while there is a soul in fetters I am not free."[3] And there was no mere hint but a very explicit statement of his position in a 1914 letter to the editor of the Terre Haute *Post:* "The worst human being," he wrote, "is still too good to be locked up in the best penitentiary as now conducted."[4]

But, in the 1922 articles which became *Walls and Bars*, a full exposition of Debs's ideas on prisons is presented. The Socialist leader was eager, in spite of his poor health, to write the articles about his prison experience because of his opportunity to push for penal reform. Prison inmates, he pointed out in the introduction to *Walls and Bars*, "are not the irretrievably vicious and depraved element they are commonly believed to be, but upon the average they are like ourselves, and it is more often their misfortune than their crime that is responsible for their plight." If prisoners were treated as they should be, he insisted, most of them, "instead of being diseased, crazed and wrecked morally and physically under a cruel and degrading prison system, would be reclaimed and restored to society, the better, not the worse for their experience."[5]

Debs was rather cynical in his introduction about the guarantee not to use the articles for propaganda purposes that the Bell Syndicate demanded of him, and he found it very difficult to separate the problem of prisons from the larger problem of capitalist society. The capitalist press was being cautious, he maintained, because it was very much aware of this close connection. "Any intelligent understanding of the prison system as it now exists, based upon a true knowledge of the graft and corruption which prevail in its management, and of the appalling vice and immorality, cruelty and crime for which the prison is responsible and of which the inmates are the helpless victims, would inevitably mean the impeachment of our smug and self-complacent capitalist society at the bar of civilization, and the utter condemnation of the capitalist system of which the prison is a necessary adjunct, and of which these rich and powerful papers are the official organs and mouthpieces."

The prison, to Debs, was "essentially a capitalistic institution," mainly for the poor. "The owning and ruling class hold the keys of the prison the same as they do of the mill and mine. They are the keepers of both and their exploited slaves are the inmates and victims of both." In fact, although his book was concerned with making prisons more bearable for their inmates, Debs really believed that it was not enough to reform the prison; he insisted that prison should be abolished "as an institution for the punishment and degradation of unfortunate human beings."[6] Debs admitted that attitudes toward criminals had softened over the years and that prisons were not nearly as bad as they once had been. But there were many things that needed to be done, "and it is for the purpose of causing to be corrected some of the crying evils that obtain in present day prisons and making possible such changes in our penal system as will mitigate the unnecessary suffering of the helpless and unfortunate inmates that I set myself the task of writing these articles before I turn my attention to anything else."[7]

Walls and Bars is poorly organized and repetitious, as is often the case with books composed of chapters originally written as separate pieces. Although much of the material relates to Debs's prison experience, he makes a number of important points throughout the book that need to be considered. Conditions in the jails and prisons of America were of particular interest to him, and he refers to this subject many times. Most prison officials, especially the guards, he maintained, seem to want to impress upon the convict that they are "wholly disinterested in the human equation, in the natural impulses that make us what we are." They try to appear "as unhuman as possible," and this ambition frequently results in inhuman treatment of prisoners.[8] Debs was especially concerned about the guns on the walls and the clubs carried by the guards which he saw as "the signs and symbols of the prison institution" proclaiming "its cruel function to the world." He firmly believed that both types of weapons should be eliminated from prisons. "To the extent that they serve at all," he wrote, "it is in a brutalizing way which tends to promote rather than restrain attempts to escape, and causes lesser infractions of the prison discipline." Debs felt that guards should be men who were able to "control the prisoners in their charge through respect for their character instead of through fear for the clubs they carried. A man who can command the respect of other men only because he holds a club in his hand is totally unfit to be in any position of authority in the outside world, much less so in a prison." Debs was convinced that convicts could be better controlled and their morale improved "without the club to remind them that they were under its rule and were subject at any time to its use in regulating their conduct."[9]

Debs had other complaints about prison conditions. The food was bad and ought to be improved.[10] The encouragement of "stool pigeons" was an evil that needed to be eliminated.[11] And one of the chief factors that made the prison an inhuman institution was the monotony. "It is this daily and continuous monotony," he wrote, "that dulls the brain of the prisoner, saps his initiative, very often in his youth, undermines his health, and lays the foundation for his physical and mental deterioration and final ruin."[12] These conditions existed, Debs maintained, because of insensitive, disinterested, and sometimes corrupt officials. "The fundamental evil in the present prison regime," he declared, "is that the institution is under the control of office holders and politicians who, even if they had the inclination, have not the time to concern themselves with prison affairs."[13]

The Socialist leader regarded a prison warden as one who occupied a more important position than a college president. But, while the college president was chosen with some care and concern about his qualifications, "the warden is usually awarded his office in return for his political services irrespective of his fitness to hold a position that has to do with the welfare of human beings."[14] All too frequently, corruption complicated the picture. This was one of the reasons, according to Debs, that the food was so bad. It would never be improved, he maintained, "until direct and effective measures have been taken to eliminate the graft of one kind and another in the contracts under which the food is furnished, and in the handling of the food inside the walls from the time it is delivered until it is served to the convicts."[15]

Debs also charged that county sheriffs often delayed the release of prisoners because the sheriffs were paid by the county for feeding the prisoners—and the more prisoners in their cells, the higher their income. This system also tempted the sheriffs to lower the quality of the meals so that a substantial portion of the food allotment could go into their own pockets, Debs implied.[16] Lawyers engaged in corrupt practices, keeping clients in county jails longer than was necessary under the pretext that they were not ready for trial, that more evidence had to be found, "when as a matter of fact the mercenary lawyer in his craven heart knows he is seeking, not for evidence with which to liberate the defenceless victim but to extract the last possible penny from the man in jail before he is railroaded beyond his reach to the penitentiary."[17]

Such neglect, brutality, and corruption were all the more regrettable to Debs because, in his constant search for the good in man, he found the inhabitants of the jails and prisons to be anything but the depraved creatures that they were thought to be by the general public. He had nothing but good words for his fellow convicts whom he saw as victims of a vicious society. In any prison, he maintained, one could find a cross section of society; the inmates "in point of character, intelligence and habits, will compare favorably with any similar number of persons outside of prison walls."[18] The intensity of Debs's love for his fellow man was never more clearly revealed than in his account of his treatment by his cell mates at Atlanta. He told of one who gave up his lower bunk to Debs when, as the newest member of the group, the Socialist leader should have occupied an upper. This same convict made Debs's bed so that it would pass inspection and even did his laundry. "I was never more free in my life, so far as my spirit was concerned," he wrote, "than I was in that prison cell. There was never a harsh or an unkind word spoken in that little community. . . ." Although his cell mates were convicted felons, Debs declared, "in their ministrations to me and to each other in their unselfish desire to give rather than receive, and in their eagerness to serve rather than be served, they set an example that might well be followed by some people who never saw the inside of prison walls." In the little community that these convicts had created in their cell, "there was not the slightest trace of a criminal, and the brotherly relation to each other, and the condition from which it sprang precluded the possibility of crime or criminal intent from entering that voluntary prison brotherhood."[19]

Thus Debs believed that convicts were basically good men and that the primary object of prison ought to be to rehabilitate them. Not only did the individual convicts deserve rehabilitation but society in general would be the beneficiary. "We should bear in mind that few men go to prison for life," he wrote, "and the force that swept them into prison sweeps them out again, and they must go back into the social stream and fight for a living." But rehabilitation was not the main goal of prison officials; instead, a dehumanizing process often destroyed prisoners, especially when they were forced to serve long sentences: "When a man has remained in prison over a certain length of time his spirit is doomed. He is stripped of his manhood. He is fearful and afraid. He has not been redeemed. He has become a roving animal casting about for prey, and too weak to seize it. He is often too weak to live even by the law of the fang and the claw. He is not acceptable even in the jungle of human life, for the denizens of the wilderness demand strength and bravery as the price and tax of admission."[20]

Debs was especially concerned about people, particularly young people and first offenders, who, unable to furnish bail, were held in jail for long periods while awaiting trial. It was bad enough for those who were eventually convicted of the charges against them, for their time in jail before trial did not count toward their sentence. But, even if they were found innocent, Debs wrote, "an irreparable injury has been done them by society, not only in point of moral contamination, but in branding them as jail birds, the record of which is ineffaceable and might as well be stamped upon their foreheads. That record will follow them through every avenue and lane of life and will serve to convict them in advance of any charge that any malevolent person might subsequently bring against them." And, emphasizing the fact that jails frequently launch young people on a career of crime, Debs called upon society to "pause long and consider well before putting the boy in jail for the first time,— especially the boy who has not the few dollars that are sometimes necessary to keep him out of jail." The Socialist leader suggested that, if accused persons were trusted to appear when needed, few would betray this confidence—"and far better it would be should such rare instances as a betrayal of confidence occur, than that a single innocent boy should be lodged in jail and given a police record and started on his criminal career. In such a case a crime is indeed committed, a crime of cruel and tragic consequences, and society itself is the criminal."[21]

Debs's attitude toward prisons and convicts was not disassociated from his Socialist analysis of society, for he was firmly convinced that the capitalist system was responsible for filling the prisons. Most crimes for which men were imprisoned, he pointed out, were crimes against property; and, under the capitalist system, "there is far more concern about property and infinitely greater care in its conservation than in human life." Moreover, the rampant poverty found in capitalist society was an important factor in sending men to prison. A large majority of convicts were in prison because they did not have enough money to hire top lawyers and to finance interminable legal delays. Debs declared that "there are a thousand ways in which the man with money who is charged with crime may escape at least the prison penalty from the moment that his bail money keeps him out of jail and through all the myriad technicalities his purse will permit him to take advantage of. . . ." He was convinced that if poverty could be abolished, the prison would no longer be needed for it is "cornerstoned in the misery, despair and desperation that poverty entails."[22]

Debs was optimistic about eliminating prisons because he was optimistic about the triumph of Socialism; for such a society would mean freedom for all, including freedom from poverty. "What incentive would there be for a man to steal when he could acquire a

happy living so much more easily and reputably by doing his share
of the community work?" he asked. "He would have to be a perverted product of capitalism indeed who would rather steal than
serve in such a community." For Debs believed that men do not
object to working; they object to working primarily for the benefit of
someone else. This factor would not occur under a Socialist system
in which no man would have to work to enrich the idle capitalist; for,
as he pointed out, "the idler will no longer own the means of life. No
man will be an economic dependent and no man need feel the pinch
of poverty that robs life of all joy and ends finally in the county
house, the prison and pottersfield." And, when poverty had disap-
peared, he wrote, "the prison will remain only as a monument to the
ages before light dawned upon darkness and civilization came to
mankind."[23]

While Debs was obviously confident that a day would come when
prisons would be superfluous, even the optimistic Debs knew that
such a day was a long way from dawning and that, in the meantime,
something needed to be done about reforming the prisons which
were going to exist for a while. In a most interesting chapter of *Walls
and Bars*, Debs wrote about how he would manage a prison if given
the chance. He would, in the first place, remove its control from
politicians and put it under a board of resident men and women "of
the highest character, the humanest impulses, and the most
efficient qualifications for their tasks." He would also organize the
prison population "upon a basis of mutuality of interest and self-
government" and eliminate not only the guns and clubs but also all
guards. In Debs's prison, the convicts would choose their own
guards from among themselves, for he felt that they were "the only
ones interested in making the prison clean and keeping out
'dope'. . . ." Food and food service would, of course, be improved.
The Socialist leader was convinced that sufficient funds were provided by the government for adequate food in federal prisons, "but
there is a wide space between the treasury from which the money is
drawn to the table upon which the food is served, and in the present
process the food deteriorates sadly in various ways before it reaches
the convicts." The prison board would have to supervise this area
carefully to eliminate graft and to see that the food was properly
cooked and served.

Self-rule was the keystone of Debs's plan. For instance, he would
reorganize the industrial life of the prison by making more use of

convicts in positions of authority. Under the prison board, a subordinate body chosen by the convicts would direct activities. "It might be necessary to employ a few experts or specialists from the outside," he wrote, "but nearly all the minor official positions in the offices, shops, yards, cell-houses and about the grounds and walls could and should be filled by the inmates." Not only in the area of work did Debs propose to have the convicts direct their own activities. His scheme involved the organization of all convicts into a parliament, and the drawing up of a code of by-laws and regulations approved by the prison board. An executive council made up of convicts would meet daily "to receive suggestions, to hear and determine complaints, subject to appeal to the governing board, and to have general supervision and direction of affairs within the prison." Whether or not this executive council is the same body that would direct the industrial activities of the prison is not made clear.

Debs would solicit suggestions and support from the convicts themselves about the proposed changes, and he was convinced that they would be approved by an overwhelming majority of the inmates. "This would be a direct appeal to their honor, their self respect, as well as their intelligent self-interest," he wrote, "and there would be few indeed who would fail to respond with gladness of heart." The Socialist leader was certain that his reforms would not only be widely acclaimed by the convicts; they would make for better prisons. If given a chance to put them into effect in any prison in the United States, he guaranteed "to greatly improve the morale of the prison the first week, to reduce the practice of immoral, health-destroying habits, and the admission of 'dope' to the minimum; increase the efficiency of the service, reduce materially the expenses of maintenance, and return the inmates to society in a different spirit and appreciably nearer rehabilitation than is now done or possible to be done under the prevailing system."

Debs never missed an opportunity to put in a plug for Socialism, which he seldom lost sight of regardless of his immediate concerns. Thus, after this dissertation on prison reform, Debs could not resist concluding the chapter with a statement that "the economic and social ideals which I hold . . . would, if once realized, not only reform the prison and mitigate its evils, but would absolutely abolish that grim and menacing survival of the dark ages." If only Socialism—the great panacea!—would come to pass, none of his elaborate plans for prison reform would be needed.[24]

II *Women*

Debs could soar to tremendous heights in his praise of womanhood, and nowhere is this tendency more apparent than in an article
entitled "Woman" which appeared in *The Bulletin* during his imprisonment at Atlanta. He could not think of woman "without a
feeling of reverence that amounts almost to worship. . . . If man the
titan makes the world big, woman the enchantress makes it beautiful. If man finds the food, it is the woman that brings the babe
through paths she sets with roses, and it is she who makes shining
and sweet the gateway when the soul fares forth alone to the un-
known land." Considering what woman had done for the world,
Debs felt ashamed to think what man had done to her: "He has filled
her delicate hands with burdens she could not bear, and laid upon
her shoulders weights that crushed her to the earth, and though she
stumbled on uncomplainingly, kissing the hand that smote her, he
has taunted her as an inferior and ruled her as if she were a slave."
Woman had invented all the arts; and, "without her divine ministrations, all things would speedily lose their charm."[25]

Debs came close to surpassing his *Bulletin* effort on another occasion, this time in a pamphlet published by the Socialist party entitled *Woman—Comrade and Equal*. He began by referring to a
statement that he had recently read which declared that man's
superiority was shown by his ability to keep woman in subjection.
Such sentiments infuriated Debs who regarded them as "the voice
of the wilderness, the snarl of the primitive. Measured by that
standard, every tyrant has been a hero and brutality is at once the
acme of perfection and the glory of man." Although woman "has not
reached the full height which she might attain . . . ," Debs, continued, man had also not reached his best and never would "until he
walks the upward way side by side with woman. Plato was right in
his fancy that man and woman are merely halves of humanity, each
requiring the qualities of the other in order to attain the highest
character. Shakespeare understood it when he made his noblest
women strong as men and his best men tender as women."[26]

The position of women in capitalistic society was a sorry one
indeed, Debs maintained: "She does not vote, she has no voice and
must bear silent witness to her legally ordained inferiority." Regarded as the property of man, she is "governed by him as may suit
his convenience." In addition, while she has to compete with man,
she has to accept lower wages when she works outside the home.[27]

Debs was especially concerned about the girls who were driven to prostitution which he regarded as "a necessary part of capitalistic society."[28] In an article entitled "Fantine in Our Day," which appeared in the *International Socialist Review* in 1916, Debs made use of Victor Hugo's heroine in *Les Miserables* to discuss his own views on prostitution: "Fantine—child of poverty and starvation—the ruined girl, the abandoned mother, the hounded prostitute, remained to the very hour of her tragic death chaste as a virgin, spotless as a saint in the holy sanctuary of her own pure and undefiled soul. . . ." To Debs, many modern Fantines were "branded as 'prostitutes' and shunned as lepers." But there were no "prostitutes" among upper-class women, Debs pointed out. Even though there were sexually immoral women, they were not called "prostitutes" or "fallen women."

But let a poor shop-girl, a seamstress or a domestic servant—in a word, a working girl—commit some slight indiscretion, and that hour her doom is sealed, and she might as well present herself at once to the public authorities and have the scarlet letter seared into her forehead with a branding iron. She may be pure and innocent as a child, but the "benefit of the doubt" never fails to condemn her. She has "gone wrong," is now a "fallen woman," and the word "prostitute," coined exclusively for her, now designates the low estate which is to be her lot for the rest of her life.[29]

When, in 1913, the daughter of an old Terre Haute friend was arrested for immorality, Debs got himself appointed temporary probation officer and took the girl into his home. In his defense against the public condemnation of his deed, he declared that "there is but one thing remarkable about opening our home to an unfortunate young woman, and that is that anyone should consider it remarkable. This fact is significant. Persecution of these unfortunate girls is the rule, and so common that it attracts no attention. Kindness is so exceptional that it provokes widespread comment." Such women were usually not wicked, he insisted; they were "sick and suffering" and in need of care, sympathy, and love.[30]

Such, to Debs, was the state of women under capitalism. With the victory of Socialism, of course, all would change. A veritable utopia for women would come into being. "In Socialism," Debs wrote in 1904, "woman would stand forth the equal of man—all the avenues would be open to her and she would naturally find her fitting place and rise from the low plane of menial servility to the dignity of ideal womanhood."[31] Some years later he wrote in a similar manner: "Socialism . . . will . . . open all the avenues equally to all the women of the world, giving to each the fullest opportunity for growth, development, expansion, the greatest possible usefulness, and then woman's work will count for all it is worth, her influence will strengthen, refine and ennoble the race, and her achievements will dazzle the world."[32] Debs did not agree with those Socialists "who dismiss the whole question of woman's political rights as a mere incident in the social revolution." Rather, he insisted that "woman's fight to have her political disability removed and to be given the rights of a human being and the standing of a citizen is a vital issue of itself and . . . it is the duty of every socialist to champion their cause. . . ."[33]

Besides, women could help achieve the Socialist victory. Debs believed that capitalism must be defeated with the democratic process, and this process meant that votes would be needed. He seemed confident that large numbers of women would vote for Socialism. "An aroused, enfranchised, enlightened womanhood," he declared, "will ultimately sweep into oblivion every agency of human oppression that today blocks the way to the emancipation of the race. . . ."[34] On another occasion he declared that, when equality of the sexes is achieved "and the working woman takes her place side by side with the working man all along the battlefront[,] the great struggle will soon be crowned with victory."[35]

Women would be particularly useful as campaign workers, Debs believed. "As this campaign develops," he wrote of the 1908 presidential contest, "the need for every available comrade to serve in the ranks will press upon us and one of the greatest will be for women on the rostrum and [in] the field as speakers and propagandists. There are certain advantages which women have over men which give their work special influence of a character which is sorely needed at this time." He told of one instance when he watched a Socialist woman address a street crowd: "Her eyes sparkled, her cheeks glowed and her voice was vibrant with enthusiasm. It was an inspiration to me. She held the crowd close to her while she drove home her telling points." People tended to pay particular attention to a woman, Debs believed, "and when she is animated by Socialist principles and ideals she at once becomes a power in molding thought and in starting the crowd on the right track. Most earnestly do I hope to see every woman who understands Socialism and is in position to speak for it out on the hustings when the campaign opens."[36]

Thus, for a number of reasons, the emancipation of women was important to Debs. Not only did their contributions to civilization warrant equal treatment with men, but they could be useful in bringing about the highly desired Socialist victory both as voters and as party workers.

III *Black Americans*

Important, too, was the Black. Surely a man who was so overflowing with compassion for his fellow man could not fail to want to improve the lot of the Afro-American. Although this subject was not one to which Debs devoted a great deal of space in his writings and his speeches, there is no question about his general concern. As early as the middle 1880's when he was a member of the Indiana House of Representatives, he supported, unsuccessfully, a bill to abolish distinctions of race and color in Indiana laws.[37] And in 1895, while serving his term in the Woodstock jail, he called for organized labor to "learn the power of and the imperative necessity of a united ballot, and in this is meant the ballot of all who work for their daily bread without regard to color or sex."[38]

Later, in 1903, Debs spoke out even more forcefully on the racial question. "For myself, my heart goes to the Negro and I make no apology to any white man for it," he wrote. "In fact, when I see the poor, brutalized, outraged black victim, I feel a burning sense of guilt for his intellectual poverty and moral debasement that makes me blush for the unspeakable crimes committed by my own race."[39] In another article written the same year, he declared that "all my life I have opposed discrimination, political, economic or social, against any human being, on account of color or sex, regarding all such as relics of the ignorant, cruel and barbarous past."[40]

Debs firmly believed that the plight of the Black should be a topic of concern for the Socialist party, and he disagreed with those party members who wished to have nothing to do with it. When, in 1903, he set forth his views in "The Negro in the Class Struggle" in the *International Socialist Review*, he was rebuked by a Socialist who believed that "you will jeopardize the best interests of the Socialist Party if you insist on political equality of the Negro. . . . If the resolutions are adopted to give the African equality with the Anglo-Saxon you will lose more votes than you now think. I for my part shall do all I can to make you lose as many as possible and there will be others." Debs reprinted this letter with a reply in a subsequent issue of the *Review*, and he made clear his belief that the party should support the Black. After chiding the writer for his anonymity, Debs declared that ". . . the Socialist Party would be false to its historic mission, violate the fundamental principles of Socialism, deny its philosophy and repudiate its own teachings if, on account of race considerations, it sought to exclude any human being from political equality and economic freedom."[41]

In spite of Debs's obvious sympathy for the Black, he did not make him a primary subject for his writings and speeches because he saw the racial question, not as a unique problem that cried for a unique solution, but as part of a larger whole. The Black was only another worker; and, if the problem for all workers—essentially an economic problem—were solved, the problem of the Black would be solved as well. "It is not a question of white labor or black labor, or male labor or female labor or child labor in this system," he declared in a speech that inaugurated his first presidential campaign in 1900; "it is solely a question of cheap labor, without reference to the effect upon mankind."[42] And in the 1903 *International Socialist Review* article, he wrote that, "properly speaking, there is no Negro question outside of the labor question—the working class struggle. Our position as Socialists and as a party is perfectly plain. We have simply to say: 'The class struggle is colorless.' The capitalists, white, black and other shades, are on one side and the workers, white, black and all other colors, on the other side."[43] Debs firmly believed that "the negro is not one whit worse off than thousands of white slaves who throng the same labor market to sell their labor power to the same industrial masters."[44] "We have nothing special to offer the Negro," he insisted, "and we cannot make separate appeals to all the races."[45]

Debs was not in agreement with the views of Booker T. Washington, the foremost Black leader of the day who sought to cooperate with white industrialists, and who cautioned his fellow Blacks to proceed slowly, to concentrate on economic advance and on vocational education rather than on social and political rights. Although Debs had "great consideration" for Washington and believed that "his motive is doubtless pure," he was convinced that Washington's "blood is still tainted with reverence for and obeisance to the master, and he does not seem to realize that the auction block and slave pen differ in degree only from the 'labor market.'" Debs was disturbed because the Black leader was supported by the "plutocrats" who furnished funds for Tuskegee Institute. He believed that, "if it were conducted with a view of opening the negro's eyes and emancipating him from the system of wage-slavery which robs and debases him while it fattens his master, not another dollar would be subscribed for the negro's 'industrial education.'" The Black did not seek charity, Debs maintained; he sought "industrial freedom"—and, when he achieves that, "he will attend to his own education."[46]

During the presidential campaign of 1908, the Negroes' National League abandoned its support of the Republican party; and its president asked Debs for a statement showing the attitude of the Socialists toward the Blacks. This request gave the Socialist leader another opportunity to express at some length his sentiments on racial matters. "I am in hearty sympathy with you in so far as your organization seeks the political and economic freedom of the negro race," Debs replied. "The people of your race are entitled to all the rights and opportunities that other races are entitled to, but they have never had them, nor will they ever have them under the administration of either the Republican or Democratic party."

Debs mentioned in the letter the Brownsville affair which was threatening to turn Black voters away from the Republican party. Two years earlier, in Brownsville, Texas, three companies of Black soldiers were allegedly involved in a riot that resulted in the death of a citizen and in injuries to others. An investigation found the Blacks to blame for the riot, and President Theodore Roosevelt dismissed the whole batallion without honor, declaring that they could never again be members of either the military or civil service of the United States. The decision was met with a great uproar among Blacks who felt that such severe punishment should not have been administered without a fair trial. The controversy did not completely subside for several years, and one of its immediate effects was to turn Blacks against Roosevelt.

Debs regarded the Brownsville affair as "disgraceful and indefensible," but he did not believe that the situation was due to racial discrimination. Once again returning to his position that the racial problem was only part of a larger problem inherent in the capitalistic system, he stated that "it is not a question of race, but a question of class. The white workingman is no higher in the present social

scale than is the negro, and although the prejudice of the one against
the other is assiduously cultivated by the ruling class, that class has
no more real regard for a wage slave of one color than of another. . . ." When capitalism is abolished and when the Blacks are given
economic freedom, the Socialist leader declared, "the race question, as it menaces capitalist class society will be known no more."

Debs pointed out that the Socialist party was working to awaken
the Black worker to the truths of Socialism and had several Black
organizers at work. But he wanted to make clear that the Socialist
party was interested only in those Black votes which were given
freely by those who knew what a vote for Socialism meant. "If the
Socialist party could by the trickery and fraud employed by the
Republican and Democratic parties," he wrote, "obtain the entire
vote of the six hundred thousand negroes for whom you speak it
would scorn to stoop to that base level." The Socialist party was
aware that most Blacks were ignorant, but it refused to take advantage of that ignorance: "The Socialist party wants every negro vote it
can get, provided it represents the intelligence, dignity and honesty
of the man who casts it. The Socialist party does not invest in whisky
and cigars as a means of influencing the votes of negroes or others,
nor does it spend a single cent to influence any man's vote except as
that vote can be influenced in an educational way."[47]

Although Eugene Debs had great compassion for the Black
American and felt that the Socialist party should be concerned about
the racial problem, his solution was overly simplistic, even naïve.
This naïveté was made painfully evident when he wrote in 1903 that:
"The Socialist party . . . is abosolutely free from color prejudice,
and the labor union . . . is rapidly becoming so, and in the next few
years not a trace of it will remain even in the so-called black belt of
the southern states."[48] Debs's anonymous correspondent of that
year showed very clearly that not even his party was "absolutely
free" of prejudice, and the Socialist leader's prediction of the early
demise of racism in the United States was obviously wrong. Debs's
view of the racial question underscores the poverty of a single-
minded emphasis on economic determinism as a causal factor; his
reliance on this view obviously blinded him to the deep-seated
racism in American society which was at the heart of the racial
problem—and was to remain for years after Debs's death.

CHAPTER 8

Religion, Education, Government

THERE are three remaining categories of ideas to which Eugene
Debs gave some attention in his writings and speeches. None
was of paramount importance to him, for nothing could sway him
from his primary focus on the need for economic change. Yet religious thinking was not alien to him, education was a matter of some
concern, and he saw important transformations in government inevitably accompanying a victory of Socialism. Thus, Debs's ideas in
these three areas need to be considered.

I *Religion*

Karl Marx's famous dictum that religion is the opium of the
people has left Socialists everywhere open to the charge of atheism,
and American Socialists have been no exception. Debs provided
plenty of ammunition for those marksmen who sought to bring the
Socialist movement down on the charge of godlessness. Debs's failure to associate himself with any church and his many hard words
about churches and churchmen added support to the popular view
that the victory of Socialism would mean the death of religion. But
to deny that Debs was a religious man is either to be ignorant of
what he had to say or to define the word "religious" much too
narrowly. Atheist he was not; and, although he vacillated about
some religious principles, he seems to fit best into the tradition of
American religious liberalism. Indeed, many of his religious ideas
show a marked resemblance to those of the eighteenth-century
Deists.

There is no question about the fact that Debs had little use for the
institutionalized religion of his day, and his attitude was undoubtedly in part the result of an early life spent outside the church. His
father was Protestant and his mother Roman Catholic; and, by the
time Debs was born, neither was a churchgoer. His only personal

experience inside a church, which occurred when he was about fifteen, no doubt had considerable influence upon his attitudes toward churches and churchmen, and it so impressed him that he was able to recall it late in life. He told of visiting a Roman Catholic church in his home town of Terre Haute, Indiana, and of listening to the priest sermonize on the subject of hell. "He pictured a thousand demons and devils," Debs said, "with horns and bristling tails, clutching pitchforks, steeped in brimstone, and threatening to consume all who did not accept the interpretation of Christianity as given by the priest. I left that church with rich and royal hatred of the priest as a person, and a loathing for the church as an institution, and I vowed that I would never go inside a church again."[1]

This view of the church and churchmen did not change fundamentally as Debs grew older, and it was not confined to the Roman Catholic church. In 1886, while editor of the *Locomotive Firemen's Magazine* and long before he became a Socialist, Debs, in an editorial, took issue with the Reverend T. DeWitt Talmage who had made the claim that the church would correct the wrongs done to workingmen. There was a distinction to be made, Debs declared, between the church and Christ's religion. After quoting the Golden Rule, he wrote: "That is Christ's religion. That is the gospel chart and lighthouse. But nowhere on God's green earth does the church obey the injunction." He then expressed his view of Talmage:

Mr. Talmage deals in *gush*, in *bosh*, in *flap doodle*. He is not practical, not even sensible. The workingmen of America do not propose to wait until the church gets ready to do what it never did do. . . . We have no desire to criticise the church. It doubtless has a mission, but if it is to see that justice is done workingmen, it has yet to demonstrate that fact. In the meantime let Labor agitate and unify, vote and instruct, mass all its mighty energies for right, truth and justice, and then church or no church, the great fundamental principles of Christ's religion will be established, and the coming of Labor's millenium will be hastened.[2]

The lavishness of many churches in the face of widespread poverty was one of the reasons for Debs's frequent attacks on organized religion. In 1887, he complained that the churches "expend so much on steeples, stained glass, carpets, velvets and gilt-edged bibles, and pay such salaries to their pastors, that nothing is left for the poor."[3] Several years later, he wrote that religious organizations "profess to represent the teachings of Jesus Christ, the friend of the poor and the scathing denouncer of the rich, and yet they erect palatial buildings, dedicate themselves to the worship of Christ, and place a price upon the seats in these sanctuaries that no workingman can pay, and thus deliberately do what they can to establish an aristocracy in religion and seek to throw the responsibility of their vulgar pride upon one who was poorer than the foxes that have holes or the birds of the air that have nests."[4]

Debs was especially displeased because, in spite of what church leaders professed, the true spirit of Christ was missing in the churches. Too frequently, he felt, the churches of his day were aligned with the capitalists against the workingmen and the Socialists. On one occasion in 1902, the failure of the churches to support a strike in Terre Haute led Debs to call attention to the fact that

from no single Christian pulpit has there come in this sore hour a note of cheer. No, not one. The church is true to its historic mission. It has ever been on the side of the oppressor. There it stands today. When a rich and soulless corporation assaults its weary, worn, half-homed, half-fed work-ingman, the pulpit is as dumb as death and no echo of the voice of Christ is heard in the temple that profanes his name.

Can any doubt where the living Jesus would stand in such a struggle? Dare any one of the ministers who profess to preach his gospel represent him truly and speak as would the Master were he in Terre Haute to-day? . . . Like all who work for wages the ministers of the gospel have to serve their earthly masters. . . .[5]

At another time, in 1916, Debs attacked preachers, along with politicians, as "the real betrayers of the people, the hypocrites that Christ denounced and for which he was crucified; the slimy, oily-tongued deceivers of their ignorant trusting followers, who traffic in the slavery and misery of their fellow-beings that they may tread the paths of ease and bask in the favors of their masters."[6]

When, in 1913, Debs was criticized for helping a prostitute by taking her into his home, he lashed back at his critics by invoking the real spirit of Christ. "Every scarlet woman in the daylight is a living certificate of the Christian church's denial of Jesus Christ," he wrote. "He did not scorn and banish the erring sister. He loved and pitied her, gave her new life and new hope and rebuked without mercy the pious, heartless hypocrites, guilty of her persecution." Prostitutes were usually not wicked, he maintained, but needed care and kindness. "No man who refuses to open his home and his heart to an unfortunate and persecuted woman is a follower of Jesus Christ. He may cry 'Lord, Lord,' but he is a hypocrite."[7]

Debs was particularly vehement in his denunciation of ministers who attacked Socialism as atheistic. They were "pious misfits," most of whom had "never read a chapter of Socialist economics and are utterly ignorant of what Socialism really means, or else, knowing what it means, deliberately misrepresent it to receive the 'well-done' and the stipend from their masters." Such persons were not fit to speak in the name of religion: "They are full of cant and glibly parrot their creed, but of real religion, the spiritual influence which exalts man and consecrates him to the loving services of his fellow man, they are as barren as the arctic region is of sunflowers. Christ knew them perfectly and denounced them as hypocrites."

Debs denied that Socialists sought to destroy religion; rather, they were trying to "destroy the conditions that make true religion impossible." He maintained that it was "the veriest sarcasm to talk about religion in the cannibalism of the present system in which men devour each other like hyenas. . . . Never until this brute struggle for existence is ended and our industrial life is organized on a basis of democratic mutualism will religion come to abide with men, not the religion of creeds written in books, but the religion of deeds written in the hearts of men whose brethren are all mankind."[8] Christianity would be natural under Socialism, Debs believed, "For a human being loves love and he loves to love. It is hate that is unnatural. Love is implanted deep in our hearts, and when things are rearranged so that I can help my fellow man best by helping myself, by developing all my skill and strength and character to the full, why, then, I shall love him more than ever; and if we compete it will be as artists do, and all good men, in skill, productiveness, and good works."[9]

As in the case of the previously mentioned Reverend Talmage, Debs did not shrink from singling out ministers and attacking them by name. The execution of a murderer by a clergyman "fittingly named Robb," who happened to be a sheriff as well, brought forth a sound condemnation by the Socialist leader: "A nation that believes in capital punishment . . . is simply a nation of barbarians, and if such a nation calls itself a Christian nation, the shame is all the deeper and blacker by adding hypocrisy to the atrocious crime."

Because Robb had also been a chaplain in France during World War I, Debs made use of the occasion to attack the support of the war by ministers. "How many of these rampant warriors of the cloth," he asked, "these pious followers of the lowly and gentle Jesus who turned their pulpits into filthy sties of the profiteering pirates and screamed for war and blood—how many of these Christian clergymen who betrayed the Prince of Peace they profess to worship, had their own legs torn off, their own eyes gouged out, their own bowels ripped from their bodies?"[10]

A much better-known minister of the day, Lyman Abbott, the editor of *The Outlook*, was also the object of Debs's wrath. His fellow Socialist, Upton Sinclair, had written the book *The Profits of Religion* that exposed the church as, in Sinclair's words, "a Source of Income and a Shield to Privilege."[11] Among others, Sinclair attacked Dr. Abbott, and Debs heartily approved. After the book's publication in 1918, Debs wrote to Sinclair congratulating him for "unmasking hypocrites in high places and telling the naked truth about the superstitions, frauds and false pretenses which masquerade in the name of religion. . . . You made a very proper example of that arch-hypocrite, that pious, shameless pretender, Lyman Abbott, who prates about 'Christian Ethics' while he reeks with the filthy subsidies of his filthy masters."[12]

In view of such language, it is understandable that Debs was regarded by many as an irreligious man. And yet one does not have to look very closely at the evidence that already has been presented to see that the charge is not valid. However, a more systematic examination of the positive side of his religious outlook needs to be made. To begin with, there is little question that he believed in a God but his conception of God seemed to undergo change throughout his lifetime. And, in several ways, Debs's God bears a resemblance to the God of the Deists. Like them, Debs placed great emphasis on the idea of God as the creator of finite existence—as in, for instance, this statement made in the *Locomotive Firemen's Magazine* for March, 1883: "God scoops out great hollow places in the solid earth and fills them with the rushings of many waters. He heaps up mountains of rock and between them places the fruitful valleys. With His finger he traces the courses of mighty rivers, and above and around all places the storm riven atmosphere. We call this handiwork earth. Millions of ages ago He sent it whirling into space around its central luminary, and there it still swings, swiftly, silently, grandly, held by nothing but the eternal will of its Creator."[13]

On another occasion he wrote that "the Creator of the Universe made the flowers as certainly as the stars. . . ."[14] Man, Debs believed, was "the masterpiece of God's creation, and bearing the impress of the Creator on his soul. . . ."[15] And of all categories of men, the worker provided the raw material for God's finest creation. "Like the rough-hewn stone from which the noble statue is chiseled by the hand of man," Debs wrote, "the Toiler is the rough-hewn bulk from which the perfect Man is being chiseled by the hand of God."[16]

Debs was not consistent in his view of the part played by God in the affairs of men after the creation, but in this area also he frequently sounds like a Deist. He was fond of quoting a line from Shakespeare, as he did in a *Locomotive Firemen's Magazine* editorial of April, 1885: " 'There is a divinity which shapes our ends, rough hew them how we will.' "[17] Thus it would appear that Debs believed not only in God as creator, but also as the shaper of man's destiny. Yet, if one reads the same magazine one year later, one finds Debs quoting this line only to criticize it rather harshly: "Are we to understand by this that fate, inexorable and relentless, fixes irrevocably the destinies of men? That is to say, are we to accept the logic (?) that if a man commits murder, or theft, or any other crime, a 'divinity shaped his ends,' and that he has simply obeyed the decree of 'divinity,' whatever that may be? If we accept such conclusions, the whole superstructure of responsibility falls. We throw the entire responsibility upon 'divinity,' 'Providence,' 'fate,' or anything else that may be convenient."[18]

In this context Debs was concerned about railroad accidents, and was not willing to allow those whom he felt were negligent to evade their responsibility by invoking "God's will." On another occasion, he wrote in a similar vein: "It has been the policy of railroads from the first, to saddle the responsibility of accidents largely upon Divine Providence, and the greater the damage to life, limb and property, the more loudly have railroad managers insisted that Divine Providence was responsible. But when the courts have taken hold of the facts for the purpose of meting out even-handed justice, Providence has been relieved of its burdens to a very large extent, and the railroads have been required to pay."[19]

This belief that God must not be blamed for what man does on earth is supported by another statement Debs made a few years later. "I do not believe everything is ordered for the best, nor for the worst," Debs wrote, "in fact I do not believe things are ordered at all, by an overruling providence."[20] However, this statement is not his last, for Debs did not adhere to this point of view. When he accepted his first nomination for the presidency in 1900, he returned to the Shakespearian line; and this time he did not criticize it. "Never in all of my life," he declared, "was I so profoundly impressed with the conviction that there is a 'divinity that shapes our ends, rough-hew them how we will.'"[21] And this belief he seems to have retained; for, as the end of his life approached, he is reported to have said: "When I was much younger I used to believe that people had the will to determine the course their lives would take. I have no such illusions any more. I know that I am a creature of circumstances, and that I have had very little to say about the course my life has taken. It seemed to be laid out for me, and I merely followed in a path already cut. I think that most of us do that."[22]

Perhaps the clearest statement of Debs's ideas about God appears in an article entitled "Jehovah and God" which was published in *The Melting Pot* in 1916. There are times when men feel discouraged, he wrote, but, if at such times, "we can realize our kinship to the God of Love and Truth and Righteousness, and feel his omnipotent power pulsing in our veins, the vitalizing current of life and hope and energy renewed from the infinite reservoir speedily restores our strength, revives our hope, renews our faith and courage, and turns our ignominious defeat into glorious victory." He then clarified his concept of God: "The God I worship is the God who strengthens my strength in the war for the weak; the God who taught me how to love and serve and suffer; the God of Infinite Love who never damned a mortal soul, but gave to every living creature his divine pledge of eternal love and salvation."[23] Debs does not describe the God of Calvin, but God nevertheless. These words could hardly have been expressed by an atheist.

Debs's belief in laws superior to those made by man represents another link to the Deists and their support of the natural-law doctrine. In 1890, at the same time that he was repudiating any belief that things are ordered by an "overruling providence," he asserted that it was better to believe in "certain immutable laws."[24] Later he elaborated on this view: "The higher law of righteousness, of love and labor will prevail. It is a law which commends itself to reasoning men, a primal law enacted long before Jehovah wrote the decalogue amidst the thunders and lightnings of Sinai. It is a law written upon the tablets of every man's heart and conscience. It is a law infinitely above the creeds and dogmas and tangled disquisitions of the churches—the one law which in its operations will level humanity upward until men, redeemed from greed and every debasing ambition, shall obey its mandates and glory in its triumph."[25] This theme is not one that Debs dwelled upon, but nothing in his writings and speeches indicates that he ever renounced the higher law concept.

Debs's attitude toward Jesus is also in line with the thinking of the Deists. It is unlikely that he believed in the divinity of Christ, but there is no question about the fact that he had high regard for Jesus as a more than ordinary man and that he made frequent reference to him. Thus in a lauditory obituary of Denver clergyman Myron W. Reed (Debs did not despise all churchmen), Debs referred to Reed's sympathy as being "as tender and profound as that of the man of Galilee."[26] Christ appealed chiefly to Debs as a radical who had great sympathy for the downtrodden, and he most frequently referred to him as a champion of the poor. "The revolutionary Savior always and everywhere stood with and for the poor; . . ." Debs wrote in 1902.[27] He often invoked the name of Jesus to support the Socialist cause, and he saw the persecution of Socialists in the twentieth-century United States as similar to that of Jesus. The charges that had been brought against the Socialists were not new, Debs declared: "The Great Soul of Galilee was not only reviled but nailed to the cross by the pharisees two thousand years ago for his incomparably loving and loyal devotion to the lowly and oppressed."[28]

While Debs's concept of God seems to have undergone considerable alteration over the years, his high regard for Jesus remained unchanged. Toward the end of his life, the Socialist leader spoke of Jesus as being "not always meek and lowly, but a full red-blooded, vibrant Jewish agitator, who could hate injustice and rebuke those who oppressed the poor and exploited and robbed them."[29] Whether or not Jesus was divine, whether or not he ever actually existed, was not important to Debs as he indicated in the *Christian Socialist* in 1915: "Even if granted, for the sake of the argument, that Jesus is a pure myth, that he never really existed at all, it must still be conceded, I think, that he is today, beyond question, the greatest moral and spiritual force in the world, a force essentially and uncompromisingly revolutionary and making unceasingly and increasingly—in spite of all attempts to divert and corrupt it—for the kinship of races, the democracy of nations, and the brotherhood of men."[30]

Debs made clear his conception of Jesus as a proletarian revolutionary in his article "Jesus the Supreme Leader" that appeared in the March 1, 1914, issue of *The Coming Nation.* The Socialist leader did not care to enter into the controversy over whether Jesus was born in Nazareth or in Bethlehem. What was important to him was the fact, "about which there is no question," that Jesus was born in a stable, for this made clear his "proletarian character." The birth was divine, Debs went on, only in the same way that every other birth is divine. The immaculate conception he characterized as a "beautiful myth," and Jesus was divine only in his "Fullness and perfection . . . as an intellectual, moral and spiritual human being." Debs deplored the attempt made since the time of Jesus to make him into something that he was not and to deny what he really was; "the master proletarian revolutionist and sower of the social whirlwind. . . ." He looked upon Jesus as a loyal member of the working class who "hated and denounced the rich and cruel exploiter as passionately as he loved and sympathized with his poor and suffering victim." Jesus, he felt, was organizing a working-class movement and preparing for a working-class revolution. "Pure communism was the economic and social gospel preached by Jesus Christ," Debs wrote, "and every act and utterance which may properly be ascribed to him conclusively affirms it. Private property was to his elevated mind and exalted soul a sacrilege and a horror; an insult to God and a crime against man." To support this view, Debs referred to the fact that, under the teaching of Jesus, his disciples gave up their possessions and "'had all things in common.'" The Socialist leader concluded with warm words of praise:

> Jesus was the grandest and loftiest of human souls—sun-crowned and God-inspired; a full-statured man, red-blooded and lion-hearted, yet sweet and gentle as the noble mother who gave him birth.
> He had the majesty and poise of a god, the prophetic vision of a seer, the great, loving heart of a woman, and the unaffected innocence and simplicity of a child.

This was and is the martyred Christ of the working class, the inspired evangel of the downtrodden masses, the world's supreme revolutionary leader, whose love for the poor and the children of the poor hallowed all the days of his consecrated life, of his death, and gave to the ages his divine inspiration and his deathless name.[31]

A revolutionary, Jesus fought for the poor, for brotherhood—and he was certainly not a figure to be rejected by a Socialist—by one who considered himself to be a twentieth-century champion of the poor and of human brotherhood.

The subject of religion would not be fully treated if Debs's views about immortality were not examined. This topic is not one in which he seemed to be vitally interested, for it is not encountered frequently in his writings and speeches. This fact is not surprising, for Debs was a man very much concerned with this world. However, he did consider the question of life after death, and he seems to have changed his mind on the subject during the course of his life. In 1906, he expressed the view of an agnostic on the matter of individual immortality when he wrote in the *Chicago Socialist* in response to a question that he did not know whether "my personal, identical, conscious self shall continue to live after my body goes back to dust. . . ." He did believe, however, "in the immortal life of humanity as a whole, and as my little life merges in and becomes an elementary part of that infinitely larger life, I may, and in fact do, feel secure in the faith and belief in immortality."[32]

Closer to the end of his life, in 1922, he seemed surer of his own immortality. Again replying to a question, he answered flatly, according to the interviewer's recollection: "I believe in immortality. In spiritual consciousness beyond the grave." But Debs's mind had not changed about the *importance* of living after death. He did not care, he declared, whether "there will be any popular sentiment for me after my clay is put away . . .; I never give that a single thought. I am interested in living the fullest life that I know how to live on this earth; and I do that with moderate success because I am constantly aware that the joy that fills my cup to the brim comes from my belief that I am of some social use in the world and have contributed to the best of my ability to the happiness of my fellowmen."[33] Clearly, Debs remained devoted to living a good and useful life on earth; the prospect of immortality, although he came to believe in it in his later years, was not of primary importance to him.

Although religion was hardly central to Debs's life, he was a deeply religious person in his own way. If he frequently denounced churches and churchmen, it was only because he felt that a true religious spirit was lacking in them. Jesus Christ may or may not have been divine, but he represented a great moral and spiritual force, and his teaching and example ought to be followed; in fact, that they were not followed was the source of much of the misery that infested the world. In a sense, Debs, because of his championing of the poor and his pursuit of human brotherhood, could very well be considered a better Christian than many ardent churchgoers.

II *Education*

Even less central to Debs's thinking than religion was formal education; but he did, on occasion, express views on the subject. For the most part, when he used the word, he was referring to the education of the workers in the beliefs of Socialism, an effort which he saw as the primary task of the Socialist movement. "The campaign of the Socialist Party," he wrote during his second run for the presidency in 1904, "is and will be wholly educational. To arouse the consciousness of the workers to their economic interests as a class, to develop their capacity for clear thinking, to achieve their solidarity industrially and politically is to invest the working class with the inherent power it possesses to abolish the wage system and free itself from every form of servitude, and this is the mighty mission of the socialist movement."[34]

A year later he stated in a speech that the "primal need of the working class is education. By education I mean revolutionary education; the kind that enables men to see that the twenty-odd millions of wage-workers in the United States are wage-slaves; . . . that they must unite. . . ."[35] When the Industrial Workers of the World was formed in 1905, Debs regarded it as "essentially an educational organization" which would teach the workers "the complete operation and control of the industry in which they are employed."[36] Earlier, it will be remembered, in planning his Social Democracy of America, Debs placed considerable emphasis on education; but it was again, the kind of education one more generally associates with propaganda, since he spoke of having a newspaper, a book and pamphlet department, and a printing plant to make literature available to the members.[37]

When Debs discussed a more formal education, while not opposed to it, he was less enthusiastic and more critical. Some of his statements leave him open to the charge of anti-intellectualism, although one should be wary of pasting such a label on a person who placed so much reliance for the future of mankind on new ideas. In 1886, in the *Locomotive Firemen's Magazine*, Debs was highly critical of formal education in the United States. True to the American tradition of pragmatism, he referred to the educational system as "ornamental rather than useful." The people seemed to think that "the more 'book-learning' you can cram into a youth the better he will be able to uphold the institutions of his country." As a result of this attitude, Debs maintained, thousands of graduates from schools discovered "that they cannot knead their knowledge into bread, that to get a living in this rough and tumble world is an immensely practical business, in which there is precious little demand for the ornamental but a ceaseless requirement for the practical. . . ."

Debs bemoaned the fact that "public sentiment is afflicted with the Greek and Latin craze. If a choice is to be made between Greek and Latin, which is regarded the higher pursuit, and brick laying, stone cutting, plumbing, locomotive building, or any other mechanical pursuit, which is rated *lower*, it will be found that Greek and Latin, which stand for the professions, will bear off the palm." The American educational system, Debs believed, "is impregnated with the idea that work is degrading, and American youth are educated to avoid it." He felt that more attention should be directed to trade schools and that "there must go forth from home and school influences to counteract the vicious idea that mechanical pursuits are less honorable than the so-called 'learned professions'. . . ."[38]

A similar position, one also smacking of anti-intellectualism, was taken by Debs in the February, 1888, issue of the *Locomotive Firemen's Magazine* when he stated that, although intelligence was necessary to make effective use of the ballot, intelligence was not to be equated with "book learning," and it was "not confined to those who claim great universities as their Alma Maters." He admitted, however, that "a certain amount of education is required to enable men to comprehend the full measure of their rights, and to understand the methods by which they should be secured."[39]

The foregoing views were articulated during Debs's more conservative years; and, as has been seen, many of his ideas changed later. But in 1896, after the Pullman Strike and his incarceration at Woodstock, very close to the time of his public conversion to

Socialism, Debs still had reservations about formal education. In "The American University and the Labor Problem," his conclusion was that the university was "doing little, if anything, toward solving the 'great labor problem'" for the simple reason that "neither the American nor the European Universities were founded for any purpose directly or remotely connected with the solution of any labor problem, great or small." Universities, he believed, were aristocratic institutions inasmuch as "a University education is reserved for those who have money to purchase it, and the fact that Universities confer degrees is in itself a power employed for constituting a species of nobility . . . often as obnoxiously exclusive as a titled nobility created by kings."

The main reason the American university was not doing anything about the labor problem, Debs declared, was because it was too closely associated with the capitalistic class. It was not founded to solve labor problems, and to alter the university's objective so that it might make some effort to do so would require fundamental changes. "The American University if it would do any share in solving the 'great labor problem,'" he continued, "would be required to attack the corrupting power of money wielded by corporations, trusts and syndicates, as also the American aristocracy, whether built upon coal-oil or cod-fish, watered stocks, banks, bullion or boodle. This . . . it would not do because it is from such sources that it gets its money." At bottom, Debs was convinced, the American university had to become more democratic: "It will have to renounce all allegiances which separate it from the great body of the people and permit its colleges, if need be, to become the tombs of its errors, whether inherited or adopted, that it may in its teachings represent the American democracy rather than the American aristocracy."[40]

Debs expressed similar feelings twenty years later when he lamented that "There is no college or university in all the world for the education of masses." But this time his attitude was more positive, for these remarks were occasioned by the opening of the People's College at Fort Scott, Kansas. This institution "was founded by the working class, is financed by the working class and controlled by the rank and file of the working class to the minutest particulars." He regarded this founding of a college as a revolutionary development marking "the awakening of the masses to the necessity of establishing their own colleges and universities and educating themselves with the one supreme object of getting at the truth in all things, knowing that the truth alone can make them free and fulfill their destiny."[41]

Although the evidence is too fragmentary to enable any final conclusions, it seems that, while Debs was highly critical of and hostile to most formal education in the United States due to the fact that it did not serve the interests of the working class, he was not opposed to what he considered a proper type of formal education: "getting at the truth in all things. . . ."

III *Government*

The towering strength of Eugene Debs's economic determinism tended to leave all other determinants virtually invisible in its shadow. He was firmly convinced that the victory of Socialism would alone bring forth the millennium and that the many evils of American society would disappear if only that crowning evil, capitalism, were destroyed. Since governmental reform was regarded as incidental to economic change, the government was not one of his primary interests. Yet it was a subject to which he gave some attention in his writings and his speeches, even though it was inevitably associated with economic determinism.

In the realm of government, the courts were, without question, his chief interest and aggravation. The intervention of the courts in the Pullman Strike, which resulted in a jail sentence for Debs and other officers of the American Railway Union, initiated a long series of assaults upon the courts by the Socialist leader. One of the first appeared in 1895 while he was still in jail and while bitterness about the Pullman Strike disaster was burning in him. In a column that he was writing for the Chicago *Evening Press*, Debs struck out against the autocratic power of the courts and "the debasing methods by which certain mental and moral infirmities find their way to the bench and are permitted to don the robes of office." These judges, Debs continued,

are often the creatures of a corrupt appointing power and are selected because of their willingness to do the bidding of those who are able to pay the price of their treason to justice. Having gained notoriety as corporation lawyers, their study and ambition having been to find law for the iniquitous practices of corporations, they go upon the bench to continue their corporation practice, until men who have the means are disposed to follow the example of Jay Gould, who said: "When I want a judge I buy him."

The result of such practices is that the courts are suspect in the public eye, Debs pointed out, "because the people behold in such things only the mockery of justice. They see a petty tyrant called a judge issuing dynamite orders designed for the destruction of the rights of the workingmen and their organizations."[42]

Debs's contempt for the courts did not disappear as the Pullman Strike faded into distant memory. If there was a chance that his attitude might change, a new incident would bring forth another attack. Such was the case with the Haywood, Moyer, Pettibone affair of 1906.[43] Again, in 1909, Debs was incensed by the sentencing of Samuel Gompers and other labor leaders for contempt in the Buck Stove and Range Case. If these men were in contempt of court, the Socialist leader declared, the court "is in an infinitely larger degree in contempt of enlightened human conscience." The men were not Socialists; Debs was not in general agreement with their views; but, in this particular case, he said, "I am with them, not half-heartedly, but as thoroughly in earnest as if they were my socialist comrades, and I shall gladly give them all the support in my power." For he saw the sentence as an attack upon organized labor in general, and he called for a united protest effort by all workers so that "never again will such a decision be rendered in the United States."[44]

One of Debs's most massive attacks on the courts was occasioned by the federal prosecution of Fred Warren, editor of the *Appeal to Reason*. On January 7, 1911, Debs devoted the entire front page of the *Appeal* to an article which called for a revolt against the courts. "The working class can no longer submit to the lawless despotism of the capitalist courts in the United States," he wrote. "The only alternative left to them is revolt." Debs directed much of his outrage against the federal courts whose members, he believed, were "graduates from the legal departments of the great corporations" and who were chosen for life-time appointments by big business rather than by the people. He regarded the United States Supreme Court as "the most irresponsible and lawless body in the land" because it exercised its absolute power "with less regard for the law and greater contempt for the people than any other court on the face of the earth." To Debs, the "despotic" power of the Supreme Court had no basis in the Constitution or in any other valid source; "but [it] has been deliberately usurped, stolen, criminally appropriated, without a shadow of authority or consent from the people. . . ." Thus, when the people revolt against the court, he said, it would not be a lawless act "but in obedience to law and to vindicate the law which has been outraged, and to rebuke the recreant judges who have perverted the law to defeat the ends of justice, destroy liberty, strangle the voice of protest, and bind the people in slavery."[45]

Debs's attitude toward the courts, especially the Supreme Court, did not change in his declining years. Fourteen years after the Warren case, the aged, ailing Socialist leader was still complaining. Under capitalism, he declared in 1925, "the courts, like other social institutions, are class concerns and controlled absolutely, so far as vital, fundamental issues are concerned, by and for the class in power." As usual, he directed much of his attention to the United States Supreme Court whose power, he was convinced, had grown steadily. "The Czar of Russia in his palmiest days never had greater power over his subjects than has the Supreme Court today over the people of the United States," he wrote. He still regarded the justices of the Supreme Court as "the attorneys of the rich, the retainers and servants of the owning class . . ." who could not be expected to change their allegiance when they became judges. His immediate concern was the child-labor law which had recently been struck down by the Supreme Court—a decision that would never have been made had the law been favored by the "mill owners, manufacturers and child-sweaters. . . ."[46] In July, 1926, only a few months before his death, Debs prepared another blast—this time at the supreme court of Massachusetts about the Sacco-Vanzetti case. "The decision of this capitalist judicial tribunal is not surprising," he wrote. "It accords perfectly with the tragical farce and the farcical tragedy of the entire trial of these two absolutely innocent and shamefully persecuted working men."[47]

Although reference to the United States Senate is harder to find in his speeches and his writings, Debs detested the Senate as much as he did the courts, and for the same reasons: it was controlled by big business for the benefit of big business. In a diatribe which does him no credit as a writer, entitled "The Senate Nuisance—Abolish It" and written in 1915, the Socialist leader made very clear his feeling about that legislative body which he called "the diseased vermiform appendix of the decadent political state of capitalism. There is no more need of it than there is for a tail to an oyster or a wart to a clam." From the time of its establishment, the Senate was intended to "defeat democracy and thwart the will of the people."

The senators themselves were a "bunch of burnt-out corporation humpty-dumpties," and "a couple of husky hoboes ought to turn the hose on the bunch and sweep them into the Potomac where they might display their senatorial courtesy and talk themselves to death."[48] Debs did not present an erudite thesis in political science but the kind of clear, forceful, impassioned statement that he had made so often in his campaign to turn the people to Socialism.

As Debs suggested in some of his statements about the courts and the Senate, he was not pleased with the United States Constitution. In 1895, before his official conversion to Socialism, and long before 1913 when Charles Beard's *An Economic Interpretation of the Constitution of the United States* changed the thinking of many Americans about the Constitution, Debs expressed a desire to see that document replaced. Shortly before his release from the Woodstock jail, he replied to a question put to him by *The Chicago Sunday Tribune*, "What Would You Do If You Had $250,000,000?" Among other things, Debs answered, he would pay the expenses of a new constitutional convention to draw up a document "that no Supreme Court, at the behest of corporate capital, could make a thing of national and international contempt—a Constitution based upon the principles embodied in the Initiative and Referendum, the Imperative Mandate, and Proportional Representation."[49]

Later, he wrote the somewhat more elaborate piece "Why We Have Outgrown the United States Constitution" for *The Progressive Woman.* In it, he pointed out that the Constitutional Convention of 1787 was composed of male members of the upper class; neither workingmen nor women were in attendance. The democratic spirit embodied in the Declaration of Independence had largely subsided by 1787, he declared, "and nothing was further from the purpose of the delegates than that the government they had met to establish should be controlled by the people." As Debs saw it, the Constitution was not a democratic document; it had been imposed upon the people by a minority ruling class to keep the majority "in slavish subjection." It was "a democracy in name and form; a despotism in substance and fact!"

But, even if all that its supporters claimed for the Constitution had once been true, the Socialist leader went on, "it is now antiquated and outgrown, and utterly unsuited to the conditions and inadequate to the requirements of the present day." The population had increased, an agricultural and mercantile country had become an industrial country, and great social changes had occurred. Although industrial and social development had not been stopped by the Constitution, "these forces sweep past it with scant regard for its ancient and musty respectability." The original Constitution had to be replaced by a new one framed by representatives of the working class—including women.[50]

Debs did not go into detail about the type of government that he wanted, but it is clear that he would have built into a new government more democratic safeguards than were provided in the United States Constitution. It is quite possible that Debs did not expend much energy working out details because of his conviction that the defeat of capitalism would remove most of the problems associated with the government. With the victory of Socialism, there would be no more big businessmen to influence and corrupt judges and senators; and the pernicious power of capitalists was, after all, the main reason government had failed to serve the interests of the people as a whole. It is not surprising, therefore, that Debs conceived his main task to be to convince the American people that they should use the existing government to bring about a fundamental change in the economic system and, therefore, the government. He never really moved away from a basic position stated on the occasion of the celebration of Independence Day in 1895. "The question may be prudently asked," he declared, "What remains worth saving of the liberties of Americans? I answer—the Ballot. It is a powerful weapon if the American people can be persuaded to unify and wield it in defense of their rights and liberties."[51]

CHAPTER 9

A Final Word

IT seems appropriate to conclude this study of Eugene V. Debs by considering briefly some of the attitudes toward him held by recent historians and to make an assessment of his place in history. Particular attention needs to be given to those areas in which historians have found him wanting and to the dispute that has developed over whether he should be ranked among the liberals or the radicals in the American experience.

I *Debs and the Historians*

The emphasis on the positive achievements of Debs in this volume should not obscure the fact that he has been frequently criticized by both his admirers and his detractors for making major mistakes. One such error, in the opinion of a number of writers, was his failure to assume effective leadership of the Socialist party. Because of his dislike for conventions and party infighting and because he preferred to remain above the battle and to concentrate on carrying the Socialist crusade to the people, Debs left the party leadership to others who commanded less attention from the public at large. Not until close to the end of his life, when the Socialist party had lost much of the strength and vitality which characterized it through the first two decades of the twentieth century, did Debs accept a party office. Thus historians are led to conclude that, inasmuch as he refused to give his active support to either the right or left wing of the Socialist party, he missed a golden opportunity to bring a much-needed cohesion to the organization—a cohesion which, perhaps, would have averted its virtual demise in the 1920's. Debs was, as H. Wayne Morgan indicates, "perpetually between two fires, radical socialism and evolutionary socialism. Had he chosen to exercise the power represented by his following he no doubt could have dominated the party. . . ."[1] Veteran Socialist writer Bert

Cochran feels that the left wing, which tended toward syndicalism and violence, "could have been straightened out by Debs, who had a better feel of the American labor movement, and a superior understanding of the all-round nature of the political struggle for socialism."[2]

Perhaps Debs did shirk his responsibilities to the Socialist party. Such things are difficult to determine with certainty, but no assurance can be given that a more active role by Debs in party affairs would have had the effects suggested. Would he really have been able to unite the left and right wings if he had tried? Could he have "straightened out" the left wing as easily as Cochran believes? And how would all of this, even if successful, have affected the future of the Socialist party? Only if Debs could have prevented the decline of that party would it have been significant, and so many other factors were involved in that decline that it is difficult to see how Debs could have prevented it. One cannot help wondering, for instance, if the most diligent efforts of Debs would have prevented the split in 1919 that led to the formation of the American Communist parties. No doubt he should have worked harder at being a leader in every sense of the word, and it is unlikely that it could have done his party any harm. But one must be cautious about claiming that more vigorous activity on the part of Debs within the Socialist party would have effected miraculous cures for the ailments of that organization.

Debs has also been criticized for his attitude toward the Black. Although an unquestioned foe of racial discrimination, his preoccupation with economic determinism prevented him from comprehending the full dimensions of racism in America. He insisted that the Black's problem was identical to the problem of every other poor man in America regardless of race. Improve the Black economically by bringing into being a Socialist state, he insisted, and all of his problems will be conquered. Debs "believed that it all reduced itself to the labor question," Cochran writes. "He did not understand the responsibility of socialists to champion the specific fight for Negro equality."[3] The Socialist leader certainly failed to see that the question of race, although closely associated with economic status, is much more complex—that, while the Black's situation can be improved by more and better jobs, the matter in all its ramifications cannot be resolved until racism is defeated.

One might, perhaps, excuse a lesser man for the stand Debs took and say that, for the period, his attitude was the best that could be expected. For, after all, Debs was certainly no friend to racism; and he spoke vigorously against the plight of the Black. For others who lived in the early part of the twentieth century, such activity might be sufficient to merit praise from the enemies of racism. But Debs cannot be let off so easily. A man whose thinking in regard to women's rights and prison reform was so far advanced is expected to have better insights into the complexities of the racial problem.

Debs's difficulties in regard to the Black stem from a more fundamental failure: his single-minded belief in economic determinism which led him to see Socialism as the great panacea. The experience of the half century since his death leads one to the conclusion that his thinking was naive in many areas. "Debs saw many things too simply," Arthur M. Schlesinger has written in the introduction to *Writings and Speeches of Eugene V. Debs.* "He underestimated the American middle class and the vitality of American capitalism. His own career disproved his repeated assertion that capitalism would destroy political freedom."[4] James Weinstein, not satisfied with Schlesinger's liberal analysis, suggests a somewhat different view; but he nevertheless supports the claim that Debs was naive. Weinstein asserts that a fundamental change in the thinking of many capitalists occurred during the Progressive period, a change that Debs, as well as other Socialist leaders, never really understood. As corporations developed, business and industrial leaders became less fearful of unions—even encouraged them in the interests of stability. But Debs—whose attitudes toward the capitalist had hardened during the late nineteenth century when organized labor's struggles for higher wages and shorter hours constituted a greater threat to corporate enterprise and were, therefore, vigorously opposed—failed to comprehend fully what was happening. This failure, Weinstein contends, "was one of the things that prevented the continued growth and development of the party in the 1920s."[5]

Although a few struggling Socialist groups continue to advocate what is essentially Debs's brand of Socialism, most of those who participated in the revival of radicalism in the 1960's were repelled by big government which, they felt, Debsian Socialism could only make bigger. Debs and the old Socialists in general believed that, in a country devoted to the democratic ideal, the economy as well as the government ought to be responsible to the people. The Americans had carried through a political revolution in 1776 that had resulted in the establishment of a democratic form of government, they pointed out. Now it was time to democratize the economy. Although the virtues of giving the people more control over the economy are still recognized by radicals, the tremendous expansion of the federal government which Debsian Socialism seems to necessitate is rejected.

The naïveté of Debs in regarding Socialism as the cure-all for most of society's ills has become increasingly apparent in the nearly fifty years since his death. Socialist governments that have come into being elsewhere in the world, while at times successful by some measures, have not generally fulfilled their promise. That poverty alone does not produce social problems has been amply demonstrated by the frequency of criminal acts and by the extent of the drug problem among middle- and upper-class youths. The Watergate scandal of the 1970's suggests that, even in a government run by the people, it is difficult for them to keep things under control. It's a long climb from the bottom, where the people are, to the highest levels of government, and few of the people ever manage to get up there. What reason is there to believe that the situation would not be even worse, many radicals ask, if the government were to become still larger by taking over the major businesses in the country?

The influence that Debs has had on later generations of Americans is not easy to define with precision. Although the United States in the 1970's is far removed from anything like the Socialist system he advocated, it is a country that is much farther along the road *away* from the everyman-for-himself ethic dominant during Debs's lifetime and *toward* a system in which society feels some responsibility for its members. While Debs would not be satisfied, he could not fail to find considerable gratification in the fact that from President Franklin D. Roosevelt's New Deal onward, countless attempts have been made by the government to assist the common man and to place more power in his hands through regulatory agencies, social-justice legislation, and laws that have vastly increased the power of organized labor. If Debs were here today, he would call all of this change "reformism." He would lament the millions who still suffer, and he would urge the people to go farther—to the Cooperative Commonwealth. But his love for humanity would make him grateful for those who have benefited.

The question about Debs to be addressed at this point is how much he had to do with bringing about all of this change. It is virtually impossible to answer with any certainty, but it does not seem unreasonable to assume that his popularization of Socialism and his concern for the plight of the common man (which he so passionately conveyed to the crowds who flocked to his speeches) helped in some way to create a climate of opinion that would accept the New Deal and all the reform legislation that has come since. George Goebel, an old Socialist colleague of Debs, believed that " 'those years of education forced on the people, in towns big and little (from pulpit, platform and soapbox, by voice, leaflet and books), saved this country from civil war in the depths of depression, and gave Franklin D. Roosevelt . . . the understanding public and trained workers for the immediate job he had on taking over.' "[6] Perhaps Goebel overstates a bit the effect of Debs, but it seems likely that Debs had some such influence.

II *Debs and the American Radical Tradition*

Debs's proper place in the American tradition is not a subject upon which scholars agree.[7] It is no small tribute to him that writers representing various points on the political spectrum claim him as their own; but, as is shown below, the issue is complicated. Liberals such as Arthur M. Schlesinger, Jr., have referred to him as "a great American democrat" who stood firmly in the American liberal tradition. "The radical passions of the Jacksonians, the Free Soilers, the Populists spoke through Debs—only now in the unaccustomed vocabulary of Socialism," Schlesinger states.[8] Similarly, H. Wayne Morgan attempts to blunt Debs's radicalism by depicting him as "representative of a generation of American reformers who sought revolutionary ends by orderly and peaceful means."[9]

Other writers, especially those of a more radical tendency, resent what they consider an effort to emasculate Debs as a radical and attempt to refute this effort by emphasizing different things. Bert Cochran characterizes him as an "indomitable revolutionist" who "preached a militant class-struggle brand of socialism."[10] In his superb biography of Debs, Ray Ginger points out that the Socialist leader "clung with stubborn insistence to the basic principles of Marxian socialism."[11] And Ronald Radosh attacks those scholars who classify Debs as a liberal by arguing that Schlesinger and Morgan ignore such facts as Debs's opposition to reformist doctrines, his total commitment to revolution, and his advocacy of the right of armed, self-defense by workers.[12]

In actuality there is some truth on both sides; and this issue, like so many, can be argued either way if one is selective in his choice of evidence. Debs made thousands of statements both on the lecture platform and in print during his long career; and one can, without much difficulty, find statements that support the point of view one wishes to advocate. But a careful perusal of these utterances by a reasonably objective reader is bound to lead to the view that Debs was an ardent revolutionary. Although it is true that he was not a skilled theoretician and that his knowledge of Marxism was not profound, there seems to be little question about the fact that he grasped the fundamentals of Marxism early in his career and preached them uncompromisingly with all of his great persuasive powers to the end of his life. The urgent need to spread the doctrine of class consciousness among the workers of America and to keep the goal of Socialist revolution untarnished by the reformist tendencies of the Socialist right wing dominated Debs's existence as a Socialist.

Those who wish to claim Debs as a liberal emphasize the fact that he sought to work within the American system and that he eschewed violence. Although there is little question that, fundamentally, Debs was a man of peace and had no desire to bring about a Socialist victory in America by violent revolution, it has been shown in this study that he was quite capable of making violent statements. And, while one must recognize that he did not wish to overturn the existing economic system by violence—that he sought the victory of Socialism via the democratic process—one has to realize that he *did* want to *overturn* that system. This is not liberalism. The liberal wishes to modify, to improve the existing system that he finds inadequate; the radical seeks to replace it with an entirely new system. The difference is fundamental, and no question exists about what Debs advocated.

The controversy over where Debs belongs is only one facet of a much more fundamental disagreement between practitioners of the so-called consensus school of American historiography which developed in the 1950's and a more recent group of radical historians. Consensus historians tend to find little class division or class conflict in the American past; and, as a result, those of the consensus school who have devoted their attention to the history of American Socialism view it as alien to the American experience and as doomed to failure. If Socialism went through a period of relative success in the early part of the twentieth century, they contend, it was because the successful Socialists of that period were really reformers, not revolutionaries. The view of Daniel Bell, perhaps, expresses the consensus approach as well as any:

The socialist movement, by its very statement of goal and in its rejection of the capitalist order as a whole, could not relate itself to the specific problems of social action in the here-and-now, give-and-take polical world. It was trapped by the unhappy problem of living *"in* but not *of* the world," so it could only act, and then inadequately, as the moral, but not political, man in immoral society. It could never resolve but only straddle the basic issue of either accepting capitalist society, and seeking to transform it from within as the labor movement did, or becoming the sworn enemy of that society, like the communists. A religious movement can split its allegiances and live *in* but not *of* the world (like Lutheranism); a political movement can not.[13]

Opposed to the consensus school is a relatively new group of American historians who are not willing to regard Socialism as alien to the United States and who see it as deeply rooted in the American past. They deny that its decline was inevitable, and they point to specific factors such as factionalism and wartime persecution to explain that decline. "In large part, the failure of American socialism has been internal," writes James Weinstein. "This internal failure has contributed to the prevailing myth that there is no indigenous tradition of American socialism. . . ." Weinstein points out that "a broadly based movement for socialism did exist in the United States before and during the First World War" which "grew out of the American experience. . . ." This movement "was conscious of its traditions and was ideologically unified by a commitment to a socialist reorganization of society as the solution to the inequalities and corrupting social values it believed were inherent in American capitalism."[14]

There are, therefore, two schools of thought in Socialist historiography, one of which, in its desire to obliterate class conflict from the American experience, must explain Debs's success as due to an absence of truly revolutionary principles and must make a liberal out of him. The other, eager to show the existence of a revolutionary tradition in America, looks upon America's most famous Socialist as a powerful element in that tradition.

This study of Debs is hardly the place to attempt the virtually impossible task of rendering a final verdict in this controversy over such basic questions as the nature of American Socialism and the reasons for its decline, for much more research needs to be done before anything approaching a final answer can be given. And, yet, in order to assign Debs his proper place in history, some attention needs to be given to the matter, and some conjectures need to be made. It is difficult to understand how a country that was conceived in a revolution could have no radical tradition. Where do the efforts of the nineteenth-century Abolitionists to destroy a vicious slave system fit if not in a radical tradition? Strands of Socialist thought can be traced to the Communitarian movement that flourished in early nineteenth-century America, and these influences have roots which extend back into the seventeenth century.

Certainly Debs regarded himself and his fellow Socialists as part of a great radical tradition in America as his frequent references to the work of the Revolutionary patriots and of the Abolitionists attest. He viewed his own work as fundamentally similar to that of such men as Thomas Paine and John Brown. Thus the arguments of the consensus historians notwithstanding, there is little doubt that the American experience does have a revolutionary tradition or that Eugene V. Debs was one of its central luminaries.

It needs to be made very clear, however, that this radical tradition, especially as it applies to Debs, is very much an American tradition in that it rests on the same base as mainstream Americanism. The principles that Debs sought to put into practice were the same principles that the great majority of Americans cherish as the cornerstones of their system—equality, freedom, democracy. When he advocated the cause of women's rights, he desired to bring women into an equality with men which he believed women deserved. When he fought for industrial unionism, he sought to free from grinding poverty the masses of unskilled workers who were neglected by the craft unions of the day. When he struggled to bring about public ownership of the means of production and distribution, he wished to extend the principle of democracy into business and industry. His whole life was devoted to the expansion of these three principles—an effort made necessary because most Americans paid them lip service only.

If Debs's writings show anything, they reveal a life devoted to man—a life that anyone, regardless of political views, can admire. Unalterably opposed to militarism and war, and dedicated to the cause of rescuing workers, women, convicts, and others whom he saw as victims of the capitalistic system, Debs's optimism blazed forth for three decades, unquenched by imprisonment, by disappointing political campaigns, by poor health, and by the collapse of the movement that represented the wave of the future to him. He was not without faults. Naïve on many subjects because of his single-minded devotion to economic determinism, Debs failed to realize the full dimensions of the racial problem, and he regarded Socialism as a panacea for virtually all of society's problems. His knowledge of Marxism was not profound, and he failed to exercise effective leadership of the Socialist party. But with his superb oratorical gifts and his devotion to the cause of humanity, he represented American Socialism during its golden years. It is doubtful if any cause ever had an abler advocate.

Notes and References

(References to Debs's own works are cited without repeating his name.)

Chapter One

1. "The Miracle of Debs," in Ronald Radosh, ed., *Debs* (Englewood Cliffs, N.J., 1971), p. 141.
2. Radosh, p. 92.
3. Ray Ginger, *The Bending Cross: A Biography of Eugene Victor Debs* (New Brunswick, N.J., 1949). I have relied on this book for most of the details of Debs's life without making very many specific references to it.
4. "Youth and Action," *The Barbarian*, Oct., 1903, in the Debs Collection, Tamiment Institute Library, New York University, hereafter referred to as Debs Collection, Tamiment.
5. "My First Job," *Appeal to Reason*, Oct. 1, 1910, 3.
6. Quoted in Ginger, p. 17.
7. "Our Magazine," *Locomotive Firemen's Magazine* 7 (1883), 545. None of the editorials in this publication are signed, but it is assumed that they were written by Debs during the period of his editorship. Certainly, if he allowed these editorials to be published, he must have agreed with the ideas expressed in them.
8. "The Mission of Our Brotherhood," *ibid.*, 8 (1884), 277–8.
9. "Boycotting," *ibid.*, 10 (1886), 326–9.
10. "Strikes—Cost and Cause," *ibid.*, 10 (1886), 451.
11. "Politics," *ibid.*, 11 (1887), 3.
12. "Cause, Effect and Remedy," *ibid.*, 11 (1887), 258.
13. "The Great Strike," *ibid.*, 12 (1888), 322.
14. "Where Strikes Flourish," *ibid.*, 12 (1888), 407.
15. *Terre Haute Weekly Gazette*, Nov. 1, 1888, Debs Collection, Tamiment.
16. *Locomotive Firemen's Magazine* 10 (1886), 140.
17. *Ibid.*, p. 140.
18. "Alleged Consolidation," *ibid.*, 10 (1886), 141.
19. "Amalgamation," *ibid.*, 10 (1886), 712.
20. "Will Labor Organizations Federate?" *ibid.*, 11 (1887), 71.
21. "Fraternal Unity," *ibid.*, 12 (1888), 9.

22. "Federation, the Lesson of the Great Strike," *ibid.*, 12 (1888), 247–48.

23. "The Federation of Labor Organizations for Mutual Protection," *ibid.*, 12 (1888), 410–11.

24. "Federation," *ibid.*, 12 (1888), 811.

25. "Pullman," *ibid.*, 11 (1887), 8–9.

26. Almont Lindsey, *The Pullman Strike* (Chicago, 1942), p. 165.

Chapter Two

1. "How I Became a Socialist." *New York Comrade*, April 1902, in Joseph M. Bernstein, ed., *Writings and Speeches of Eugene V. Debs* (New York, 1948), pp. 44–5.

2. "A Great Wrong." *Locomotive Firemen's Magazine* 8 (1884), 544–5.

3. "From Obscurity to Fame," *Appeal to Reason*, Sept. 5, 1903, in Scrapbook VI, p. 88, Debs Collection, Tamiment.

4. "How I Became a Socialist," in Bernstein, p. 45.

5. United States Strike Commission, *Report on the Chicago Strike of June–July, 1894* (Washington, 1895), p. 170.

6. Laurence Gronlund, *The Cooperative Commonwealth*, ed. Stow Persons (Cambridge, 1965), pp. ix, xxi.

7. "How I Became a Socialist," in Bernstein, pp. 46–7.

8. Ginger, p. 189.

9. "Our First Great Need," Jan. 16, 1895, in Scrapbook I, p. 166, Debs Collection, Tamiment.

10. Debs to W.L. Rosenberg, *Labor*, Sept. 14, 1895, in Scrapbook I, p. 253, Debs Collection, Tamiment.

11. Bernstein, pp. 9–11.

12. Debs to the editor, Batavia, Iowa, *Sentinel*, Aug. 9, 1895, Debs Collection, Tamiment.

13. *The Railway Times*, Jan. 1, 1897, Debs Collection, Tamiment.

14. Howard H. Quint, *The Forging of American Socialism* (Indianapolis, 1953), p. 283.

15. *Ibid.*, pp. 288–89.

16. *The Western Miner*, June 12, 1897, p. 1, Debs Collection, Tamiment.

17. *The Social Democrat*, July 1, 1897, Debs Collection, Tamiment; Quint, pp. 289–94.

18. Quint, p. 313.

19. *Ibid.*, p. 318.

Chapter Three

1. Quoted in H. Wayne Morgan, *Eugene V. Debs: Socialist for President* (Syracuse, N.Y., 1962), p. 56.

2. Quint, p. 377.

3. Quoted in Ginger, p. 264.

4. See Chapter 5.

5. Debs to Ryan Walker, Aug. 5, 1912, Walker Manuscripts, Lilly Library, Indiana University.

6. David A. Shannon, *The Socialist Party of America* (Chicago, 1967), pp. 90–2; Harold W. Currie, "Allan L. Benson, Salesman of Socialism, 1902–1916," *Labor History* 11 (1970), 285–303.

7. Quoted in Ginger, p. 337.

8. Bernstein, pp. 435–36.

9. *Ibid.*, pp. 438–39.

10. Radosh, p. 139.

11. *Walls and Bars* (Chicago, 1927), pp. 124–26.

12. Bernstein, p. 452.

13. Chicago *Evening Post*, Oct. 23, 1926.

14. New York *Evening World*, Oct. 26 1926.

15. Los Angeles *Record*, Oct. 23, 1926.

16. *Ibid.*

Chapter Four

1. *The Coming Nation*, July 8, 1911, Debs Collection, Tamiment.

2. Radosh, p. 98.

3. *Ibid.*, pp. 92–3.

4. *Ibid.*, p. 141.

5. "Outlook for Socialism in the United States," *International Socialist Review*, Sept., 1900, in Bernstein, p. 34.

6. Quoted in David Karsner, *Debs: His Authorized Life and Letters From Woodstock Prison to Atlanta* (New York, 1919), p. 166.

7. "How I Became a Socialist," *New York Comrade*, April, 1902, in Bernstein, p. 44.

8. "Childhood," *Wayland's Monthly*, 1905, *ibid.*, p. 165.

9. "Industrial Unionism," Dec. 10, 1905, *ibid.*, p. 237.

10. "Woman," *The Bulletin*, April 17, 1920, p. 3, Debs Collection, Tamiment.

11. "Revolutionary Unionism," Nov. 25, 1905, in Bernstein, p. 222.

12. "Revolution," *New York Worker*, April 27, 1907, in Radosh, p. 25.

13. "Where Strikes Flourish," *Locomotive Firemen's Magazine* 12 (1888), 407.

14. *Appeal to Reason*, May 18, 1907.

15. "This Plot Must be Foiled," St. Louis *Labor*, Oct. 17, 1908, Debs Collection, Tamiment.

16. "Rescue the Refugees," *Appeal to Reason*, Jan. 2, 1909, p. 1.

17. Bernstein, pp. 434–35.

18. "Abolitionists," *Locomotive Firemen's Magazine* 11 (1887), 67–8.

19. *Appeal to Reason*, May 18, 1907.

20. "Warren Has Triumphed," *Appeal to Reason*, Dec. 10, 1910, p. 4.

21. "Voice of Truth Must be Heard," *ibid.*, Dec. 9, 1911, p. 1.

22. "The Gunmen and the Miners," *International Socialist Review*, Sept., 1914, in Bernstein, pp. 383–86.

23. Bernstein, p. 435.

24. "John Zenger and Fred Warren," *Appeal to Reason*, Aug. 27, 1910, p. 2.

25. *Locomotive Firemen's Magazine* 8 (1884), 151.

26. "Federation," Denver *United Labor*, Aug. 30, 1890, in Scrapbook I, p. 39, Debs Collection, Tamiment.

27. "The Problem of Labor," June, 1895, in Scrapbook I, pp. 214–15, Debs Collection, Tamiment.

28. Radosh, p. 12.

29. *The Railway Times*, Jan. 1, 1897, Debs Collection, Tamiment.

30. "Social Democracy," *National Magazine*, Oct., 1898, in Scrapbook III, p. 103, Debs Collection, Tamiment.

31. "Class Unionism," Nov. 24, 1905, in Bernstein, p. 209.

32. "Prison Labor," March 21, 1899, *ibid.*, p. 32.

33. "The Fight for Freedom," July 21, 1912, in *Labor and Freedom* (St. Louis, 1916), pp. 162–63.

34. Karsner, *Debs*, pp. 203–4.

35. *Appeal to Reason*, Nov. 23, 1907, in Bernstein, p. 285.

Chapter Five

1. "Employer and Employed," *Locomotive Firemen's Magazine* 8 (1884), 616–17.

2. "Politics," *ibid.*, 11 (1887), 3.

3. "Abolitionists," *ibid.*, p. 67.

4. Scrapbook I, p. 37, Debs Collection, Tamiment.

5. "Abolitionists," *Locomotive Firemen's Magazine* 11 (1887), 68.

6. "Growth of Unionism in America," American Labor Union *Journal*, Sept. 3, 1903, in Scrapbook VI, p. 88, Debs Collection, Tamiment.

7. "Craft Unionism," Nov. 23, 1905 in Bernstein, pp. 175–6.

8. "The Socialist Party and the Working Class," Sept. 1, 1904, *ibid.*, p. 128.

9. "An Ideal Labor Press," *The Metal Worker*, May, 1904, *ibid.*, p. 162.

10. "Craft Unionism," Nov. 23, 1905, *ibid.*, p. 185.

11. "The Social Democratic Party," *New York Independent*, Aug. 23, 1900, in Scrapbook V, pp. 75–6, Debs Collection, Tamiment.

12. "The Issue," May 23, 1908, in Bernstein, p. 309.

13. "Social Democracy," *Democratic Magazine*, July, 1898, in Scrapbook III, p. 163, Debs Collection, Tamiment.

14. *New York Journal*, March 7, 1900, in Scrapbook IV, p. 237, Debs Collection, Tamiment.

15. Lloyd to Debs, June 8, 1903; Debs to Lloyd, June 22, 1903, in Lloyd Papers, State Historical Society of Wisconsin.

16. "Danger Ahead," *International Socialist Review*, Jan., 1911, in Bernstein, pp. 333–34.

17. *Social Democratic Herald*, July 1, 1899, p. 1.

18. "The Barons at the White House," *The Toiler*, Oct. 10, 1902, in Scrapbook VI, p. 8, Debs Collection, Tamiment.

19. "Industrial Unionism," Dec. 10, 1905, in Bernstein, p. 233.

20. "Arouse, Ye Slaves," *Appeal to Reason*, March 10, 1906, p. 1.

21. "John Brown: History's Greatest Hero," *Appeal to Reason*, Nov. 23, 1907, in Bernstein, p. 280.

22. *Appeal to Reason*, May 18, 1907, p. 1.

23. "The McNamara Case and the Labor Movement," *International Socialist Review*, Jan., 1912, in Bernstein, pp. 345–47.

24. "The Gunmen and the Miners," *International Socialist Review*, Sept., 1914, *ibid.*, pp. 383–86; "Bravo, Arkansas Coaldiggers!" *The Miners Magazine*, July 30, 1914, p. 7.

25. Bernstein, p. 351.

26. "When I Shall Fight," *Appeal to Reason*, Sept. 11, 1915, in Scrapbook X, p. 4, Debs Collection, Tamiment.

27. "'Preparedness' and Poverty," *American Socialist*, Dec. 18, 1915, in Scrapbook X, p. 10, Debs Collection, Tamiment.

28. "The Socialist Party and the Working Class," Sept. 1, 1904, in Bernstein, p. 137.

29. "An Appeal to the Working Class," *The Toiler*, Feb.7, 1902, in Scrapbook V, p. 279, Debs Collection, Tamiment.

30. "Downfall of Capitalism," *Social Democratic Herald*, Sept. 29, 1900, p. 2.

31. "Coming of Socialism," *Studies in Socialism*, July, 1909, p. 1.

32. "Sound Socialist Tactics," *International Socialist Review*, Feb., 1912, in Bernstein, pp. 351–53.

33. *Appeal to Reason*, March 10, 1906, p. 1.

34. *Ibid.*, May 18, 1907, p. 1.

35. "Bravo, Arkansas Coaldiggers!" *The Miners Magazine*, July 30, 1914, p. 7.

36. See Chapter 6.

37. David Karsner, *Talks with Debs in Terre Haute* (New York, 1922), pp. 123–25.

38. *Ibid.*, pp. 164–65.

39. *Appeal to Reason*, Jan., 1907, in Scrapbook VII, p. 297, Debs Collection, Tamiment.

40. Lincoln Steffens, "Eugene V. Debs on What the Matter is in America and What To Do About It," *Everybody's* (1908), pp. 455–69, in Radosh, p. 115.

41. Bernstein, p. 434.

42. "The Western Labor Movement," *International Socialist Review*, *ibid.*, pp. 54–63.

43. Bernstein, p. 107.

44. *Weekly People*, Jan. 28, 1911, p. 2.

45. Debs to Miss E. H. Thomas, July 10, 1905, in Debs Mss., Indiana State Library, Indianapolis.

46. *Ibid.*

47. "Craft Unionism," Nov. 23, 1905, in Bernstein, p. 171.

48. *Ibid.*, pp. 179–80.

49. "Class Unionism," Nov. 24, 1905, *ibid.*, p. 200.

50. "Industrial Unionism," Dec. 10, 1905, *ibid.*, p. 229.

51. Debs to Tom Mann, *ibid.*, p. 329.

52. "A Plea for Solidarity," *International Socialist Review*, March, 1914, *ibid.*, pp. 368–70.

53. Bernstein, p. 406.

54. *Ibid.*, p. 431.

55. "Working Class Politics." *International Socialist Review*, Nov., 1910, *ibid.*, p. 331.

56. "A Plea for Solidarity," *International Socialist Review*, March, 1914, *ibid.*, pp. 368–69.

57. Bernstein, p. 432.

58. *New Age*, May 3, 1923, in Scrapbook SB 1–2, p. 199, Debs Collection, Tamiment.

59. "Danger Ahead," *International Socialist Review*, Jan., 1911, in Bernstein, pp. 334–35.

60. "What's Wrong with Chicago," *Chicago Socialist*, Aug. 22, 1911, in Scrapbook IX, p. 198, Debs Collection, Tamiment.

61. "Warren and Gompers," *Miners Magazine*, Dec. 22, 1911, in Scrapbook IX, p. 174, Debs Collection, Tamiment.

62. New York *Call*, Feb. 13, 1919, in Scrapbook X, p. 171, Debs Collection, Tamiment.

Chapter Six

1. "Standing Armies," *Locomotive Firemen's Magazine* 9 (1885), 472–73.

2. "More Soldiers," *Locomotive Firemen's Magazine* 10 (1886), 454.

3. "Decrease the Army," *Labor Advocate*, Dec. 10, 1898, p. 1.

4. *Social Democratic Herald*, Dec. 24, 1898, p. 3.

5. *Ibid.*

6. "War is Murder in Uniform," *The World*, March 27, 1909, p. 5.

7. "Following California's Lead," *Appeal to Reason*, Aug. 5, 1911, p. 1.

8. "'Preparedness' I Favor," *ibid.*, Dec. 11, 1914, in Scrapbook X, p. 13, Debs Collection, Tamiment.

9. "When I Fight," *ibid.*, Sept. 11, 1915, in Scrapbook X, p. 4, Debs Collection, Tamiment.

10. *American Socialist*, Dec. 9, 1916, in Scrapbook X, p. 60, Debs Collection, Tamiment.

11. Debs to Daniel Hoan, Aug. 17, 1916, Box 11, File 42, Hoan Collection, Milwaukee County Historical Society, Milwaukee, Wisconsin.

12. "When I Fight," *Appeal to Reason*, Sept. 11, 1915, in Scrapbook X, p. 4, Debs Collection, Tamiment.

13. "Preparedness and Poverty," *American Socialist*, Dec. 18, 1915, in Scrapbook X, p. 10, Debs Collection, Tamiment.

14. Debs to Sinclair, Jan. 12, 1916, Sinclair Mss., Lilly Library, Indiana University.

15. *New York Sun*, Nov. 30, 1915, in Scrapbook X, p. 9, Debs Collection, Tamiment.

16. "The Prospect for Peace," *American Socialist*, Feb. 19, 1916, in Scrapbook X, pp. 19–20, Debs Collection, Tamiment.

17. Allan L. Benson, *A Way to Prevent War* (Girard, Kansas: *Appeal to Reason*, 1915), pp. 5–6.

18. *Appeal to Reason*, April 8?, 1915, in Scrapbook IX, p. 303, Debs Collection, Tamiment.

19. "The Majority Report," *American Socialist*, May 26?, 1917, in Scrapbook X, p. 67, Debs Collection, Tamiment.

20. Bernstein, p. 425.

21. Scrapbook SB 1–2, p. 220, Debs Collection, Tamiment.

22. "The American Legion of Saviors," *Chicago Socialist*, Nov. 14, 1925, in Scrapbook SB 1–2, p. 257, Debs Collection, Tamiment.

23. "The Trumpet Call of Duty," *The Bulletin*, April, 1918, in Scrapbook X, p. 145, Debs Collection, Tamiment.

24. Bernstein, p. 424.

25. "The Day of the People," *The Class Struggle*, Feb., 1919, in Bernstein, p. 442.

26. Theodore Draper, *The Roots of American Communism* (New York, 1957), pp. 101–81, 270.

27. "Why We Are No Stronger," *Schenectady Citizen*, Dec. 17, 1920, in Scrapbook SB 1–2, p. 47, Debs Collection, Tamiment.

28. Debs to Otto Branstetter March 25, 1922, in Debs Mss., Indiana State Library, Indianapolis.

29. Karsner, *Talks*, p. 67.

30. *Ibid.*, p. 164.

31. *Ibid.*, pp. 171–72.

32. "Why We Are No Stronger," *Schenectady Citizen*, Dec. 17, 1920, in Scrapbook SB 1–2, p. 48, Debs Collection, Tamiment.

33. Karsner, *Talks*, p. 174.
34. *Ibid.*, pp. 64–6.
35. *Ibid.*, pp. 27–8.
36. Scrapbook SB 1–2, pp. 189–91; Karsner, *Talks*, pp. 32–33, 174–78.

Chapter Seven

1. "Prison Labor," *Locomotive Firemen's Magazine* 11 (1887), 1917–8.
2. "How I Became a Socialist," in Bernstein, p. 46.
3. "Between Comrades," New York *Call*, Feb., 1914, in Scrapbook X, p. 133, Debs Collection, Tamiment.
4. Terre Haute *Post*, Jan. 7, 1914, in Scrapbook IX, p. 291, Debs Collection, Tamiment.
5. *Walls and Bars*, pp. 18–19.
6. *Ibid.*, pp. 20, 23–4.
7. *Ibid.*, pp. 25, 31–2.
8. *Ibid.*, pp. 54–5.
9. *Ibid.*, pp. 131–33.
10. *Ibid.*, p. 73.
11. *Ibid.*, p. 136.
12. *Ibid.*, p. 137.
13. *Ibid.*, p. 159.
14. *Ibid.*, pp. 128–29.
15. *Ibid.*, p. 73.
16. *Ibid.*, p. 40.
17. *Ibid.*, p. 47.
18. *Ibid.*, p. 25.
19. *Ibid.*, pp. 61–2; 70–1.
20. *Ibid.*, pp. 32–3; 36–9.
21. *Ibid.*, pp. 40–4; 153.
22. *Ibid.*, pp. 172–73; 139; 142.
23. *Ibid.*, pp. 189–90.
24. *Ibid.*, pp. 166–70.
25. "Woman," *The Bulletin*, April 17, 1920, p. 3.
26. Radosh, pp. 63–5.
27. "Unionism and Socialism," *Appeal to Reason* (1904) in Bernstein, p. 122.
28. "Revolutionary Unionism," Nov. 25, 1905, *ibid.*, p. 222.
29. "Fantine in Our Day," *International Socialist Review*, March, 1916, *ibid.*, pp. 392–95.
30. New York *Journal*, July 16, 1913, in Scrapbook SB 1–1, pp. 37–8, Debs Collection, Tamiment.
31. "Unionism and Socialism," in Bernstein, p. 123.

32. "Woman's Day is Dawning," *Justice*, Feb., 1911, in Scrapbook IX, p. 161, Debs Collection, Tamiment.

33. "Women and their Fight for the Franchise," *American Socialist*, July 24?, 1915, in Scrapbook IX, p. 306, Debs Collection, Tamiment.

34. "Women and their Fight for Freedom," *ibid.*, Oct. 2, 1915, in Scrapbook X, p. 8, Debs Collection, Tamiment.

35. "Working Class Politics," *International Socialist Review*, Nov., 1910, in Bernstein, p. 333.

36. "A Momentous Campaign," *Chicago Daily Socialist*, July 3, 1908, p. 2.

37. Ginger, pp. 42–3.

38. Chicago *Evening Press*, Nov. 4, 1895, in Debs Collection, Tamiment.

39. "The Negro in the Class Struggle," *International Socialist Review*, Nov., 1903, in Bernstein, p. 66.

40. "The Negro Question," *American Labor Journal*, July 9, 1903, in Scrapbook SB 1, p. 8, Debs Collection, Tamiment.

41. "The Negro and his Nemesis," Jan., 1904, in Bernstein, pp. 66–73.

42. *Social Democratic Herald*, Oct. 6, 1900, p. 1.

43. Bernstein, p. 65.

44. "The Negro Question," *American Labor Journal*, July 9, 1903, in Scrapbook SB 1, p. 8, Debs Collection, Tamiment.

45. Bernstein, p. 66.

46. "The Negro Question," *American Labor Journal*, July 9, 1903, in Scrapbook SB 1, p. 8, Debs Collection, Tamiment.

47. Debs to J. Milton Waldron, June 30, 1908, *New York Evening Call*, Aug. 27, 1908, p. 1. In 1972, the Army cleared all of the men involved in the Brownsville affair and gave them honorable discharges. *New York Times*, Sept. 29, 1972.

48. "The Negro Question," *American Labor Journal*, July 9, 1903, in Scrapbook SB 1, p. 8, Debs Collection, Tamiment.

Chapter Eight

1. Karsner, *Talks*, p. 99.

2. "Reverend T. DeWitt Talmage on Labor Topics," *Locomotive Firemen's Magazine*, 10 (1886), 516–18.

3. "Sunday Meetings," *ibid.*, 11 (1887), 66.

4. Chicago *Evening Press*, Sept. 30, 1895, p. 2.

5. "An Appeal to the Working Class," *The Toiler*, Feb. 7, 1902, in Scrapbook V, p. 279, Debs Collection, Tamiment.

6. "Politicians and Preachers," *American Socialist*, June 24, 1916, in Scrapbook X, p. 32, Debs Collection, Tamiment.

7. New York *Journal*, July 16, 1913, in Scrapbook SB 1–1, pp. 37–8, Debs Collection, Tamiment.

8. "Prostitution of Religion," *Christian Socialist*, Dec. 18, 1915, in Scrapbook X, pp. 12–13, Debs Collection, Tamiment.

9. Lincoln Steffens, *Everybody's* (1908), pp. 455–69, in Radosh, p. 130.

10. " 'Preacher Sheriff' Hangs Victim," *New York Call Magazine*, Oct. 29, 1922, in Bernstein, pp. 446–50.

11. Upton Sinclair, *The Profits of Religion: An Essay in Economic Interpretation* (Pasadena, California, 1918), p. v.

12. Debs to Sinclair, Oct. 28, 1918, Sinclair Mss., Lilly Library, Indiana University.

13. "Man's Power and God's Power," *Locomotive Firemen's Magazine* 7 (1883), 122.

14. "May and Its Floral Wealth," *ibid.*, 9 (1885), 290.

15. "Capital and Labor," *ibid.*, p. 96.

16. "Labor Day Greeting," *Social Democartic Herald*, Sept., 1904, in Bernstein, p. 164.

17. "Expositions," *Locomotive Firemen's Magazine* 9 (1885), 219.

18. *Locomotive Firemen's Magazine* 10 (1886), 214–15.

19. "Paying Damages," *ibid.*, 11 (1887), 583.

20. "The Knights of Labor," *United Labor*, Nov. 8, 1890, in Scrapbook I, p. 40, Debs Collection, Tamiment.

21. *Social Democratic Herald*, March 24, 1900, p. 1.

22. Karsner, *Talks*, pp. 148–49.

23. "Jehovah and God," *The Melting Pot*, Feb., 1916, in Scrapbook SB 1–1, p. 50, Debs Collection, Tamiment.

24. "The Knights of Labor," *United Labor*, Nov. 8, 1890, in Scrapbook I, p. 40, Debs Collection, Tamiment.

25. "Prison Labor," March 21, 1899, in Bernstein, p. 33.

26. "Reminiscences of Myron W. Reed," *Comrade*, Nov., 1893?, in Scrapbook SB 3, p. 55, Debs Collection, Tamiment.

27. "An Appeal to the Working Class," *The Toiler*, Feb. 7, 1902, in Scrapbook V, p. 279, Debs Collection, Tamiment.

28. *Appeal to Reason*, May 1, 1909, p. 1.

29. Karsner, *Talks*, p. 63.

30. *Christian Socialist*, Oct., 1915, in Scrapbook X, p. 6, Debs Collection, Tamiment.

31. "Jesus the Supreme Leader," *The Coming Nation*, March 1, 1914, p. 2.

32. *Chicago Socialist*, Jan. 13, 1906, in Scrapbook X, p. 102, Debs Collection, Tamiment.

33. Karsner, *Talks*, pp. 142–43.

34. "The Socialist Party's Appeal (1904)," *The Comrade*, Nov., 1904, in Gene Tussey, ed., *Eugene V. Debs Speaks* (New York, 1970), p. 106.

35. "Craft Unionism," Nov. 23, 1905, in Bernstein, p. 185.

36. "Class Unionism," Nov. 24, 1905, *ibid.*, p. 200.

37. *The Western Miner*, June 12, 1897, p. 1.

38. "Trade Schools," *Locomotive Firemen's Magazine* 10 (1886), 645.

39. "Coming Events," *ibid.*, 12 (1888), 84.

40. "The American University and the Labor Problem," *The Adelbert*, Feb., 1896, pp. 167–69.

41. "The School for the Masses," *American Socialist*, Sept. 18, 1915, in Scrapbook X, p. 7, Debs Collection, Tamiment.

42. Chicago *Evening Press*, Nov. 11, 1895.

43. See Chapter 5.

44. "The Gompers Jail Sentence," *Appeal to Reason*, Jan. 2, 1909, p. 4.

45. "Declaration of Revolt" *Appeal to Reason*, Jan. 7, 1911, p. 1.

46. "Supreme Court and Child Slavery," St. Louis *Labor*, Jan. 28, 1925, in Scrapbook SB 1–2, p. 228, Debs Collection, Tamiment.

47. "Sacco and Vanzetti," *Labor Defender*, July, 1926, in Bernstein, p. 450.

48. "The Senate Nuisance–Abolish It," *Appeal to Reason*, Feb. 27, 1915, in Scrapbook IX, p. 300, Debs Collection, Tamiment.

49. *The Chicago Sunday Tribune*, Nov. 10, 1895.

50. "Why We Have Outgrown the United States Constitution," *The Progressive Woman*, Sept. 1, 1911, p. 5.

51. "Liberty's Anniversary," *Twentieth Century*, July 4, 1895, in Scrapbook I, p. 218, Debs Collection, Tamiment.

Chapter Nine

1. Morgan, p. 201.

2. "The Achievement of Debs," in Harvey Goldberg, ed., *American Radicals: Some Problems and Personalities* (New York, 1957), p. 170.

3. *Ibid.*, p. 173.

4. Bernstein, p. xiii.

5. Radosh, p. 171.

6. Quoted in Bernstein, p. xiii.

7. See Radosh, pp. 143–78 for a more extensive discussion.

8. Bernstein, p. xiii.

9. Morgan, p. 23.

10. "The Achievement of Debs," in Goldberg, *American Radicals*, pp. 166–67.

11. Ginger, p. 378.

12. Radosh, p. 174.

13. Daniel Bell, *Marxian Socialism in the United States* (Princeton, 1967), p. 5.

14. James Weinstein, *The Decline of Socialism in America, 1912–1925* (New York, 1967), pp. viii–ix. For further discussion of the writing of Socialist history, see James Weinstein, "Socialism's Hidden Heritage: Scholarship

Reinforces Political Mythology," in James Weinstein and David W. Eakins, eds., *For A New America: Essays in History and Politics from Studies on the Left, 1959–1967* (New York, 1970), pp. 221–52; Sally M. Miller, "Socialist Party Decline and World War I: Bibliography and Interpretation," *Science & Society* 34 (1970), 398–411; Bryan Strong, "Historians and American Socialism, 1900–1920," *ibid.*, pp. 387–97.

Selected Bibliography

BIBLIOGRAPHIES

EGBERT, DONALD DREW, and STOW PERSONS, eds. *Socialism and American Life.* Bibliographer, T. D. Seymour Bassett. Vol. II. Princeton: Princeton University Press, 1952. An exhaustive bibliography of American Socialism to 1952; indispensable to the student of any aspect of the subject.

GINGER, RAY, *The Bending Cross: A Biography of Eugene Victor Debs.* New Brunswick, N.J.: Rutgers University Press, 1949. Includes a long bibliography of writings by and about Debs.

RADOSH, RONALD, ed. *Debs.* Englewood Cliffs, N.J.: Prentice-Hall, 1971. Has a brief but useful bibliographical note on Debs materials.

PRIMARY SOURCES

1. *Special Collections of Debs Material*
    Unfortunately, there is no central repository where the bulk of Debs materials can be found. Those collections which appear below were the most useful in the preparation of this book. For a more complete list, see the Ray Ginger bibliography listed above.

Debs Manuscripts, Indiana State Library, Indianapolis, Indiana.

Debs Collection, Tamiment Institute Library, New York University, New York City.

Debs Collection, Debs House, Terre Haute, Indiana.

Daniel Hoan Collection, Milwaukee County Historical Society, Milwaukee, Wisconsin.

Joseph Labadie Collection, University of Michigan Library, Ann Arbor, Michigan.

Henry Demarest Lloyd Papers, State Historical Society of Wisconsin, Madison, Wisconsin.

Upton Sinclair Manuscripts, Lilly Library, Indiana University, Bloomington, Indiana.

Walker Manuscripts, Lilly Library, Indiana University, Bloomington, Indiana.

2. *Publications of Eugene V. Debs*

No attempt has been made to list separately any of the thousands of articles written by Debs, for those used in this book are cited in Notes and References. The best single source of his articles, aside from the many printed collections which have appeared, is the collection of scrapbooks kept by Debs which are now in the Tamiment Institute Library in New York City.

A. Periodicals to which Debs was a frequent contributor are: *American Socialist*, 1915–17; *Appeal to Reason*, 1906–13; *Debs Magazine*, 1922–23; *International Socialist Review*, 1900–18; *Locomotive Firemen's Magazine*, 1878–94; New York *Call*, 1908–26; New York *Liberator*, 1919–24; *Railway Times* (*Social Democrat*, 1897–98), 1894–98; *Social Democratic Herald*, 1898–1905.

B. Collections of Debs's writings and speeches:

BERNSTEIN, JOSEPH M., ed. *Writings and Speeches of Eugene V. Debs.* New York: Hermitage Press, 1948.

DEBS, EUGENE V. *Walls and Bars.* Chicago: Socialist Party, 1927.

KARSNER, DAVID. *Talks with Debs in Terre Haute (and Letters from Lindlahr).* New York: The New York *Call*, 1922.

Labor and Freedom: The Voice and Pen of Eugene V. Debs. St. Louis: Phil Wagner, 1916.

RADOSH, RONALD, ed. *Debs.* Englewood Cliffs, N.J.: Prentice-Hall, 1971.

ROGERS, BRUCE, ed. *Debs: His Life, Writings and Speeches.* Girard, Kansas: *The Appeal to Reason*, 1908.

TUSSEY, JEAN Y., ed. *Eugene V. Debs Speaks.* New York: Pathfinder Press, 1970.

UNITED STATES STRIKE COMMISSION. *Report on the Chicago Strike of June–July, 1894.* Washington, D.C.: Government Printing Office, 1895.

SECONDARY SOURCES

BELL, DANIEL. *Marxian Socialism in the United States.* Princeton: Princeton University Press, 1967. Originally published in *Socialism and American Life*, I, 213–405. Good background material; especially useful because it deals with all Marxist groups instead of focusing on one party.

COCHRAN, BERT. "The Achievement of Debs." In *American Radicals: Some Problems and Personalities*, Harvey Goldberg, ed. New York: Monthly Review Press, 1957. An essay on Debs by a Socialist who stresses the militant, revolutionist side of the Socialist leader.

COLEMAN, MCALISTER. *Eugene V. Debs: A Man Unafraid.* New York: Greenberg, 1930. Older, sympathetic biography, useful in its time; replaced by more recent works.

DICK, WILLIAM M. *Labor and Socialism in America: The Gompers Era*. Port Washington, New York: Kennikat Press, 1972. Deals with the relationship between American Socialists and the labor movement from the 1880's to 1924.

DRAPER, THEODORE. *The Roots of American Communism*. New York: Viking Press, 1957. Detailed, invaluable study of the break-up of the Socialist party and the establishment of the American Communist parties following World War I.

EGBERT, DONALD DREW, and STOW PERSONS, eds. *Socialism and American Life*. Vol. I. Princeton: Princeton University Press, 1952. Collection of essays (some very long) on various aspects of American Socialism.

GINGER, RAY. *The Bending Cross: A Biography of Eugene Victor Debs*. New Brunswick, N.J.: Rutgers University Press, 1949. Also available in a paperback edition entitled *Eugene V. Debs: A Biography* (New York: Collier Books, 1962). Finest Biography by far of Debs.

HERRESHOFF, DAVID. *American Disciples of Marx: From the age of Jackson to the Progressive era*. Detroit: Wayne State University Press, 1967. Contends that Debs represented a De Leonist influence in the Socialist party.

KARSNER, DAVID. *Debs: His Authorized Life and Letters From Woodstock Prison to Atlanta*. New York: Boni and Liveright, 1919. Early biography by a friend of Debs; valuable for views of one who knew him well.

KIPNIS, IRA. *The American Socialist Movement, 1897–1912*. New York: Columbia University Press, 1952. Detailed history from the Marxist point of view of the movement during its greatest years.

LASLETT, JOHN H. M. *Labor and the Left: A Study of Socialist and Radical Influences in the American Labor Movement, 1881–1924*. New York: Basic Books, Inc., 1970. Study of the reasons for the failure of American radicals to control the labor movement.

LINDSEY, ALMONT. *The Pullman Strike: The Story of a Unique Experiment and of a Great Labor Upheaval*. Chicago: University of Chicago Press, 1942. Best account of the Pullman Strike.

MADISON, CHARLES A. "Eugene Victor Debs: Evangelical Socialist." *In Critics and Crusaders: A Century of American Protest*, 2nd ed. New York: Frederick Ungar, 1959. Brief, sympathetic treatment of Debs as the representation of the Socialist aspect of Jeffersonian democracy.

MILLER, SALLY M. "Socialist Party Decline and World War I: Bibliography and Interpretation." *Science & Society* 34 (1970), 398–411. Useful discussion of Socialist historiography.

MORGAN, H. WAYNE. *Eugene V. Debs: Socialist for President*. Syracuse, N.Y.: Syracuse University Press, 1962. Useful study; concentrates on Debs's presidential campaigns and the political history of the Socialists between 1900 and 1925.

QUINT, HOWARD H. *The Forging of American Socialism: Origins of the Modern Movement*. Columbia: University of South Carolina Press, 1953. Able treatment of the Socialist movement in America in the late nineteenth century; especially important to the student of Debs for its account of his early career as a Socialist.

SHANNON, DAVID A. *The Socialist Party of America: A History*. New York: The Macmillan Co., 1955. First-rate account of the Socialist party from its birth in 1901 to the early 1950's.

STRONG, BRYAN. "Historians and American Socialism, 1900–1920." *Science & Society* 34 (1970), 387–97. Discussion of the development of consensus history.

WEINSTEIN, JAMES. *The Decline of Socialism in America, 1912–1925*. New York: Monthly Review Press, 1967. Disputes the widely held belief that American Socialism began to decline after the election of 1912; places the blame for the decline on internal failure.

WEINSTEIN, JAMES, and DAVID W. EAKINS, eds. *For A New America: Essays in History and Politics from Studies on the Left, 1959–1967*. New York: Random House, 1970. Includes useful articles on the decline of American radicalism and the writing of Socialist history.

Index

155